Best
Pub Walks
around Glasgow

David Hunter

Published by Sigma Leisure – an imprint of
Sigma Press, 1 South Oak Lane, Wilmslow, Cheshire SK9 6AR, England.

British Library Cataloguing in Publication Data
A CIP record for this book is available from the British Library.

ISBN: 1-85058-673-X

Typesetting and Design by: Sigma Press, Wilmslow, Cheshire.

Cover photograph: aerial view of George Square (by permission, Scottish Media Newspapers Ltd)

Maps: Jeremy Semmens

Photographs: the author

Printed by: MFP Design and Print

Disclaimer: the information in this book is given in good faith and is believed to be correct at the time of publication. No responsibility is accepted by either the author or publisher for errors or omissions, or for any loss or injury howsoever caused. Only you can judge your own fitness, competence and experience.

Preface

This book is the natural evolution of a successful series of 'Pub Walks'. As a Scotsman living in Manchester who had used and enjoyed several of these books, it seemed only natural to try to transplant the idea north of the border and the rest, as they say, is history.

Each walk includes instructions on how to find the pub where you start and finish the walk, together with information on parking. There is information about the hours of opening, the food available, the beers that are served and a brief history of the pub. To make the walk as interesting as possible, there is usually a section describing the area – information about its history, geography, wildlife or unusual features – such as walks along the West Highland Way or a visit to a distillery with free tastings!

All of the walks have been thoroughly researched and tested. Mostly, you will be on clearly-defined footpaths, bridleways, quiet lanes and canal towpaths. On the occasions that you do have to cross trackless countryside, I have attempted to guide you by reference to obvious physical features of the landscape – though it is always best to carry the appropriate Ordnance Survey map and not to depend completely on the sketch maps provided, excellent as I believe them to be. You should also know how to use a compass before venturing into the countryside.

Glasgow is remarkably well provided with accessible open country. There is the open vastness of the Kilpatrick Hills, the challenge of the West Highland Way, Ayrshire's rolling hills and sandy beaches, and the Renfrew Hills with their Roman remains. All of this within a short journey from the city centre.

The best way of all to discover Scotland is on foot. In a car you do not see a fraction of the countryside as it whizzes by at fifty miles an hour. Breathe fresh air, not exhaust fumes; look at the flowers, not at the bumper of the car in front. Touch the living bark of a tree, not the dead plastic of a steering wheel. Walking in the countryside – and especially the Scottish countryside – is interesting, enjoyable and healthy. In short, all of the best things in modern life!

David Hunter

Acknowledgements

The writer of a book is like the visible tip of an iceberg, with the other ninety per cent invisible under the water. This is to say thanks to all those unseen people who contributed so much to make this book possible. Firstly my mother for putting me up and putting up with me while I was doing the research for this book. Thanks are also due to Kate Cuthbert and her staff at Pollok Country Park. Also to Alma Topen at the brewing archives of Glasgow University. Helen Sykes gave me much valuable information about the Applebank Inn. Dave Powell at Gleniffer Braes Country Park was unstinting with time and assistance. Mr and Mrs Stewart for their help, many thanks. Alison Brown of Drymen was very helpful, as was Elma Lindsay of Stirling Library. Finally thanks and grateful appreciation to all the countryside rangers, foresters, local historians, publicans and librarians who gave so freely and generously of their time and knowledge. Special mention must be given to the staff of Burnage public library whose patience and tolerance passeth all understanding. A special mention must be given to the staff at Apex in Lane End Road, Burnage for helping with my odd photocopying requirements.

Dedication

This book is dedicated to my parents whose, hard work and self sacrifice gave their children the opportunities they never had. And to Mr. Grotte and his team and Manchester Royal Infirmary whose skill and dedication gave me my life back again.

Contents

Burns Country

Soap Opera, Scotland

The West Highland Way

'Doon the Watter'

The Clyde Valley

The Kelvin Valley

Renfrewshire

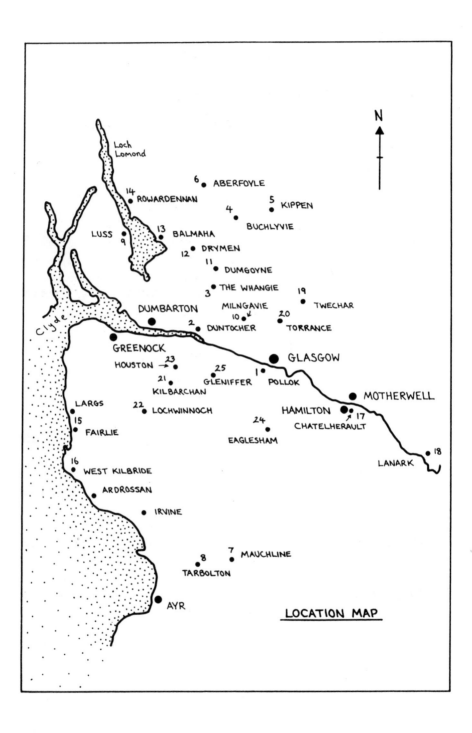

LOCATION MAP

Before you begin . . .

In Your Pack

It is always wise to carry a backpack and a few basic necessities. Food and drink are essential – it is a good idea to include instant energy food such as Mars bars or Kendal Mint Cake and these can be safely left in your pack between walks. Fruit is another good source of easily ingestible sugar and is also good for thirst if you run out of drink. You only appreciate how much juice there is in an apple or an orange when you have run out of drink on a really hot day and one of these fruits is nectar for a desiccated gullet.

As to the nature of the drink that you carry, this is a question of personal taste. Soft drinks, non-diet versions, can be a useful boost if the blood sugar levels fall. Some people carry beer, some squash and some tea or coffee, but I carry just plain water. I got into this habit while walking with a dog that would not touch lemonade or squash even if his tongue was hanging out. You can also use water to rinse your hands or face, or on a genuine scorcher you can even pour it over your head.

Always have a hat with you: in the winter it warms your head, while in the summer, in these days of ozone depletion, it protects you from the sun. You will need a warm waterproof jacket, remember that it can be much colder in the country than in the city and for every hundred metres that you climb the temperature drops by one degree Fahrenheit. Walking can quickly make you warm and you can cool quickly when you stop so it is important to be able to regulate your temperature swiftly and easily. Consequently, take two thin jerseys rather than one heavy one. Strong trousers are a good idea; you may find yourself making an unplanned excursion through brambles or barbed wire. Shorts are fine on a hot day but be sure you have something to cover your legs as the weather may change or your path may lead you through a nettle patch. Lightweight waterproof trousers can be good for this. There are few things worse than sodden jeans so I do not recommend walking in jeans. Straight-leg jeans are particularly unsuitable for walking in the country, although I wear them myself when not walking in the country.

The trouble with these is that you go over one stile too many and they rip at the crotch. I love trainers and they are brilliant for walking city streets when you seem to float along on a cloud of air, but they are not for walking in the country. You will need proper hiking boots, with ankle support in case you slip. And, with hiking boots, the cleats in the soles will make you much less likely to slip. Finally, to protect your feet, buy your hiking boots a size too large and wear two pairs of thick socks as well as boot socks. If it is good enough for the SAS yomping over the Brecon Beacons, it will be good enough for us.

You will need to carry, and to know how to use, a map and compass. In navigation there is one simple rule: God is in the details. If you glance at a map impatiently and quickly rush off I can guarantee you will soon be lost, I have done it myself many times. Peer and squint at the map, take your time, work out where you are and where you are going, and if you do not know what a symbol means look it up on the edge of the map. If you do this you will seldom, if ever, get lost.

Beers and Brewers

In pre-medieval times the Picts brewed heather- and spruce-flavoured ales. From the 12th century onwards these were replaced by practices which are the basis of brewing today and which were brought over by German monks. Hops do not grow well in Scotland because of the climate so there has been a historical preference for flavouring beers with roasted barley. This is akin to how whisky is flavoured: stopping the malting process by heating it over a peat fire.

In the past Scotland produced two main ales. One was Scotch Ale – powerful, blackish, sugary and heavy. The other was Tuppeny Ale, named after its price in 1707. This was produced by a second wash of the barley after it was used for making Scotch Ale. This was a weak or small beer. Around that time the introduction of 'common barley', as it is now known, greatly improved the quality of Scottish beers.

Brewing was traditionally a small-scale process until the markets were opened up by good commercial transport such as railways and canals. It then became concentrated in three main centres: Alloa, Edinburgh and Glasgow. Edinburgh and Alloa had good supplies of hard water and produced mostly pale ales. Glasgow has soft water and concentrated on stouts and porters. Towards the end of the 19th century brewing in Scotland tilted eastwards to Edinburgh and Alloa, and their highly hopped and decreased original gravity beers. These tended to travel soundly and keep well. These were exported to the Raj and became India Pale Ales. Scottish beer at this time made up a quarter of all beer exported from Britain. This first convenience beer could have been the start of the trend that has most people still drinking keg beers.

In Scotland the real ale tide came in and receded. But as with an incoming tide, the second wave is longer and stronger. New breweries are currently opening up faster than I can keep track of them. The major producers of real ale in Scotland are Belhaven, Caledonian Brewing, Maclays and Broughton. Belhaven is based in Dunbar and was established in 1719. The company produces a regular range of real ales plus seasonal specialities. However, not all Belhaven products are real ale. In Edinburgh, the Caledonian Brewing Company, established in 1869, makes only its award-winning real ales. Maclays of Alloa, founded in 1830, brews both real and keg ales. Their Kanes Amber Ale is a tribute to Dan Kane, a weel-kent man in Scottish cask-conditioned circles, now sadly deceased. In the Borders village of Broughton, the eponymous company creates real ale including its famed Greenmantle.

Of the smaller breweries, Harviestoun by Dollar produces only real ale and Traquair ale is also noteworthy. In 1965 the Laird of Traquair, Mr Maxwell-Stewart, commenced real ale brewing after finding a complete old brewery and equipment on his estate. This apparatus is believed to have been made in 1720. The Inveralmond brewery is based in Perth. Among other small brewers are Orkney, whose award-winning Dark Island is found throughout Scotland, and West Highland Brewers, based in an old station in Argyllshire. Independence brews in Invergordon and Stirling Bitter is a pleasant pint produced by the Bridge of Allan Brewing Company. Last but not least, the Fox and Hounds in Houston has opened its own in-pub brewery. They produce two ales: Killellan, a pale, hoppy ale, and Barochan, a darker beer with a hint of roasted barley.

Finally, if you are a stranger to Scotland you will find a confusing plethora of shilling ales ranging from 60/- to 90/-. Historically this relates to the duty payable on a barrel of beer so the higher the shilling number the stronger the beer, as a rough rule of thumb. Very crudely 60/- is alcohol by volume (ABV) 2.6 per cent to 3.7 per cent, 70/- is ABV 3.2 per cent to 4.2 per cent and 80/- is ABV 3.9 per cent to 4.5 per cent.

Access to the Countryside in Scotland

These walks encompass country parks, recognised footpaths with stiles and/or kissing gates, canal towpaths and waterworks roads, cycle routes, farm tracks, long-distance routes such as the West Highland Way, minor roads, major roads (short distances only), forest roads, open moorland (occasionally) and, rarely, rights of way. The Ordnance Survey maps seem deceptive to me. They say 'public rights of way, not applicable in Scotland', but there are a small number of rights of way in Scotland. There is also a Scottish Rights of Way Society. Its address is John Cotton Business Centre, 10 Sunnyside, Edinburgh EH7 5RA. The point is that I cannot put together a book of walks around Glasgow if I rely solely on rights of way. Such a volume would not be slim; it would be anorexic.

Historically the status quo in Scotland has been that you can walk where you like as long as you do not cause any damage. But this is common law and ambiguous. It is like the empty space in the centre of old maps that said 'here be dragons'. Insofar as I understand it, you have unrestricted access to unfenced land. Otherwise there is no law of criminal trespass in Scotland, but you can be sued in a civil court if you cause damage.

In practice you are unlikely to have any problems. Walkers are well tolerated in Scotland and the walks I have given you are all on recognised paths when across farmland. When researching this book, if I was balked or checked in any way, even by as much as a dirty look, then I abandoned the idea of that walk. I have walked all the walks in this book unhindered, and frequently found friendly people along the way. The law is being reviewed as I write this (July 1998) but I doubt if changes will be made very quickly. One point worth remembering is that when a sign says 'Private Road' this normally applies only to vehicular traffic, not hikers.

Finally, please remember the country code. Take nothing but pictures and leave nothing behind you but closed gates. Keep your dogs under close control at all times, and especially when near livestock. And remember people make a living in the countryside; it is not a theme park. So if a farmer temporarily closes a path in the lambing season respect this, it is his livelihood. And if a path is closed during the shooting season, it is your life that is being protected as well as the landowner's living.

The West of Scotland

At the beginning of recorded history this area was occupied by Cymric tribes. These Celts arrived in Britain in one of the periodic pulses of migration that had swept westwards across Europe. The Romans ebbed and flowed into this area a few times, leaving little discernible evidence apart from some roads and ruins. The Celtic kingdom was known as Strathclyde and at one point stretched as far south as Preston.

In the Dark Ages the Scots lived to the north of Strathclyde, the Picts ruled to the north-east, the Angles occupied the east, while to the south the Saxon English reigned. All Scotland was united under Malcolm Canmore in the 11th century and became known as Scotland. In the 12th century David I stiffened Scotland with Normans, whose castles and churches brought a modicum of stability. The monks in places like Lanark and Paisley taught the locals the Continental skills of weaving, spinning, brewing etc. These Normans and native Scots fought side by side in the Wars of Independence. Sir William Wallace kicked off in Lanark in the early 1290s and Robert the Bruce scored the golden goal at Bannockburn in 1314. Malcolm, Earl of Lennox, and Bishop Wishart of Glasgow were seminal figures in this. Bruce, a genius guerrilla fighter, won one of his most important battles at Loudon Hill near Kilmarnock.

Later came the Reformation and most people of the area became Protestant instead of Roman Catholic. Subsequently, King and Kirk clashed over who should appoint clergy. Troops and covenanters fought pitched battles in which many died, including those at Drumclog near Loudon Hill and at Mauchline. The Jacobite rebellions did not greatly affect this region, although Glasgow was forced to feed and clothe the Young Pretender's army.

The West of Scotland was on the right side of the country when trade opened up with the Americas. The tobacco lords of Glasgow were beyond all in pride and arrogance. They even had their own stretches of pavement on which only they were allowed to walk. Although knowing Glasgwegians, I expect that the ordinary folk passed along these pavements too. With industrialisation, many folk moved into the towns and cities to work in shipbuilding, steel, chemicals, spinning, weaving etc. Canals and railways aided the movements of goods and people. The Union blockade of Confederate ports was a blow from which the textile industry never really recovered.

Nowadays this part of Scotland is rising like a phoenix from the ashes of its dead and dying sunset industries of steel, shipbuilding etc.

and is rebuilding itself in the modern era of sunrise industries of computers, electronics and so on. Nevertheless, much of the area continues unaffected by industrial fashion and continues with its ancestral work of farming, fishing and forestry.

The people of this zone remain what they always were: tough, resilient, cheerful and uncomplaining. Glasgow is no longer the 'No Mean City' of my youth. The people of the West of Scotland are open, friendly and hospitable. Behave that way and you will get along fine. But as for poseurs and pseuds, the less said about their reception the better. If there is a phrase that sums up the 'Folk of the West' it is 'We're all Jock Tamson's bairns' – we are all God's children.

1. Pollok Country Park

Route: White Cart Water – Pollok House and Gardens – North Woods Earthworks – Burrell Collection

Distance: 3 miles

Map: OS Landranger 64, Glasgow

Start: Stoat and Ferret, Pollokshaws Road, Glasgow

Access: This walk is easily reached from the Glasgow area. By car: from the centre of Glasgow take the M8 westbound for Glasgow Airport and Greenock. Leave at junction 22 and join the M77 for Kilmarnock. Come off the M77 at junction 1 and turn left at the roundabout to join the B768 (Dumbreck Road), signposted in brown for the Burrell Collection. At the first set of traffic lights turn right onto the B769 (Haggs Road). Go through one set of lights and under the railway bridge to a set of traffic lights. At these traffic lights, built into the base of a red sandstone tenement on your left, is the Stoat and Ferret. Turn left at these traffic lights into Pollokshaws Road, which has unrestricted parking. The pub has no car park. By bus: a frequent service, for information ring the Glasgow Travel Centre on 0141 636 3195. By train: catch the East Kilbride train from Glasgow Central to Pollokshaws West station. Come out of the station and turn left along Pollokshaws Road. The main entrance to Pollok Country Park is about 100 metres on your left. There are four trains an hour Monday to Saturday and two trains an hour on Sundays.

The Stoat and Ferret

The Stoat and Ferret is, in the Glasgow parlance, a stoater of a pub. A stoater is an excellent thing. Previously called the Old Swan, it was built in 1901 as an integral part of the red sandstone tenement. As the Old Swan the pub had a bad reputation and was dirty. It was taken over by new management and renamed two years ago. Like anything or anyone with a bad reputation it has had to work twice as hard and be twice as good as anyone else. This is to the great benefit of current customers.

The pub is open 11.00 to 23.00 Monday to Thursday, 11.00 to 24.00 Friday and Saturday, and 12.30 to 23.00 on Sundays. Traditional pub food is served all day every day. A slimmed-down menu is served in the evenings, mainly Tapas-style snacks. Seven cask-conditioned ales are always available. Tetleys, Deuchars IPA and Belhaven 60/- are the regulars, with four varying guest ales from all over the country. Two stouts and cask-conditioned cider are also available. For lager drinkers there is Budweiser Budvar, brewed in the Czech city of Budweiss for the past 700 years, and the original Budweiser. There is also classical Belgian Hoegarden white beer available on draught. It is a comfortable, friendly and well-appointed pub. Telephone 0141 632 0161.

Pollok House

Pollok Country Park

This is three miles from the centre of Glasgow but has otters and salmon in the White Cart Water and roe-deer in the park and adjacent golf course. It is officially classified as countryside. The park is mainly wooded and contains, along with the contiguous Pollok Estate, farmland, golf courses, tennis, cricket, Highland cattle, police dog training, the Burrell Collection, Pollok House, many specialised gardens (rose, herb, vegetable, rhododendron etc.) and lots of other attractions.

Pollok Country Park covers 144 hectares (361 acres). Mrs Anne

Maxwell MacDonald gifted it to Glasgow and its people in 1966. Pollok
Estate has a long history with the Maxwell family. In the 1900s Sir John
Stirling Maxwell sponsored plant hunters to visit the East and received
a percentage of their seed spoils in return. Sir John and his head gardener bred many rare and unique rhododendrons, some of which still
only exist in the woodland gardens of Pollok house. The woodland garden is on the hill just above the walled garden, to the east of Pollok
House. Another rarity to be found here is the handkerchief tree. The
white bracts of the flowers of this tree resemble white handkerchiefs. In
early summer the rangers on the estate get calls from far and wide ask-
ing if it is in flower. Their number is 0141 632 9299. It normally flowers
from the middle to the end of June, but it varies according to the
weather.

The North Woods contain earthworks thought to be the remains of a
Dark Age homestead. These were partially excavated and explored in
the 1960s by a team of archaeologists from Glasgow University.

The Walk

From the Stoat and Ferret, continue further along the road that you
drove down to the pub (if you came by car). After about 100 metres you
will pass Pollokshaws Town Hall on your left. This is about 100 years
old and is a fine example of Scottish Baroque with crow-step gables. It is
currently being restored. About 50 metres past this on the opposite side
of the road is the entrance to Pollok Country Park.

Walk directly into Pollok Country Park, ignoring the path on your
right. Go past the list of attractions. About 20 metres past the gatehouse,
go left where the sign indicates a riverside walk. This path is not on the
1996 O S Landranger map. Turn left past the tennis courts, keeping
them on your right, then turn left at the end of the tennis courts. Follow
the path along the White Cart riverbank for about half a mile.

On your right you will come to the police dog training school, recog-
nisable by the hurdles in the paddock. Demonstrations are held on
Tuesday mornings between 10.00 and 11.00. When I was there in November there were a herd of Pollok Park's Highland cattle in the next
field. Their fearsome appearance belies their extremely placid tempera-
ment.

When you come to a path coming in from the right, bear left and keep
to the riverbank. The walls of Pollok House gardens appear ahead as

you keep on this path. There is a beech hedge on your left. At the end of the beech hedge, there are toilets about 20 metres off-route along the path on your right, should you need them. After the beech hedge follow the path round and to the right between buildings (signed 'water-driven sawmill').

This sawmill was originally used to process timber on the estate but around 1900 a turbine was installed which provided DC power to the house. This was used until mains power arrived in the 1930s. The sawmill is not open to the public.

Keep along the path past the weir and up to the bridge on your left. If you stand in the middle of the bridge you may be lucky enough to see a kingfisher; they breed on the estate. The flow of water over this weir in spate can reach 70,000 litres a second.

The centre of the bridge also makes a good vantage point for looking at Pollok House. This was planned by William Adam in the mid-1700s and built by his better-known son John. About 1850 Sir William Maxwell, an expert on Spanish art, acquired paintings by Goya, El Greco and Murillo, and Spanish glass. These can be seen in the house. The hill to the right of Pollok House originally had a fort on it of which nothing remains. In May and June this is covered by rhododendrons.

To reach the front entrance of Pollok House, leave the bridge and take the steps up between the two stone lions. Go diagonally right through the garden and up the stairs into the ornate pavilion at the top. This is dated 1901. Turn left into the formal garden and bear diagonally left through this. You can reach the walled garden by going straight ahead at the pavilion at the top of the stairs.

There is a gardener's bothy in these gardens, an agricultural worker's cott house, which illustrates living conditions for a gardener around 1900.

At the end of the formal garden take the stairs down to the left and into the courtyard at the front of Pollok House. (For details of opening hours etc. of the house ring the National Trust on 0131 226 5922.) From the door of Pollok House go out through the archway and up the ride between the trees directly opposite.

At the top of this ride, which is glorious with daffodils in spring, pause for breath and admire the way the ride frames Pollok House beneath you. This ride was a 21st birthday present for Sir John Stirling Maxwell from Sir Alexander Crum of Thornliebank who gave him 21 pairs of lime trees for his coming of age.

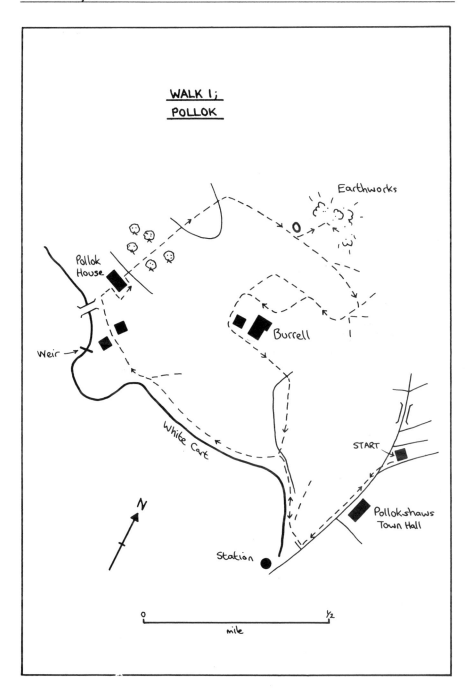

WALK 1;
POLLOK

From the top of the hill follow the path straight ahead and downhill. At the road (traffic-free) go straight ahead, keeping the large rhododendron on your right. At the next road follow the obvious path straight ahead up the hill. This path can be muddy. Follow the path around to the right until you reach a path cutting diagonally across. Go on the path diagonally on your left until you arrive at a pond. Go round the pond, keeping it on your left. At the tarmac and traffic-free road turn right for about 50 metres. On your left behind a bench are the earthworks from the Dark Ages.

Retrace your footsteps to the pond and turn left, keeping the pond on your right. Turn left on the larger path not the minor one that goes through the fence. When you reach a T-junction turn right uphill. At the four-way junction turn right and immediately right again. At this point the Burrell may be seen on your left, if there are not too many leaves on the trees. At the fork, go left downhill. This path veers to the right and runs behind the Burrell. Bear round to the left at the fork then again at the top of the hill, keeping Knowehead Lodge on your left.

Just before the Burrell, note the ornate stone drinking fountain with lions on your right. The Burrell opening hours can be obtained by ringing 0141 649 7151. It has a coffee bar and a licensed restaurant which does evening meals Thursday to Saturday (inclusive) between 19.00 and 22.00. The Burrell is a remarkable private collection of varied works of art, only a small percentage of which can be seen at any one time. The portal and doors at the entrance to the Burrell are from Hornby Castle in Yorkshire. The doorway dates from the 14th or 15th century, and the doors from the 18th or 19th. Only the carved stones are original, they are of sandstone.

Come out of the Burrell and turn left along the tarmac footpath. At the end of this path cross the road carefully (traffic!) and follow the signs to Pollokshaws Road. When this path ends, cross the main entrance road for traffic and pick up the path on the other side. Follow this to Pollokshaws Road. Turn left here and the Stoat and Ferret is about 100 metres up on your right.

2. Kilpatrick Hills

Route: Duntocher – Greenside Reservoir – Loch Humphrey – Kilpatrick Braes – Antonine Wall

Distance: 7 miles

Map: OS Landranger 64, Glasgow

Start: Duntiglennan Bar

Access: Duntocher is about ten miles to the north-west of Glasgow. By car: take the A82 out of Glasgow, signposted for Dumbarton and Loch Lomond. At the first roundabout beyond the city boundary take the A8014, on your right, to Hardgate. At the Hardgate roundabout take the A810, on your left, for Duntocher. The Duntiglennan Inn is about a quarter of a mile along on your right. If you turn right into Chapel Street just before the pub, you can then turn immediately left into the car park behind the pub. By bus: there is a regular service from Glasgow. Telephone 0141 226 4826. There are no suitable train services.

Duntocher

Duntocher is a suburb of Clydebank. The most notable part of its history was the Blitz. On two consecutive nights, the 13th and 14th of March 1941, this area was heavily bombed. 236 bombers attacked on the first night and 203 on the second night. Their targets were shipyards, Dunottar Tank Farm and ammunition producers such as Singers of Dalmuir. Pathfinders came first and dropped incendiary bombs to mark the target. Inflammable targets such as Singers timber yard and Yoker distillery acted as beacons for the bombers and were very badly hit. Non-inflammable targets of brick and metal, such as shipyards, were largely untouched. 358 people died, and gas, electricity and water were cut off.

It is a measure of the intensity of this bombing that only 8 houses out of 12,000 were left undamaged. In the small village of Duntocher alone, three churches were destroyed: Duntocher Trinity, Duntocher East (church, manse and hall) and St Mary's Church, Duntocher. At the height of the Blitz a student nurse appeared at a church hall casualty station. She commandeered an ambulance and took a badly wounded baby to the Western Infirmary in Glasgow. There she press-ganged six medical students to return with her. They succeeded, despite an exploding bomb throwing the ambulance on its side, and after many hours of heroic work they left. To this day no one knows the name of this Angel of Clydebank.

View of the Clyde, Duntocher

The Walk

Turn left out of the Duntiglennan Inn and walk along the main road for about a quarter of a mile. About 200 metres after the pub there is a hill on your right which was the site of a Roman fort. This was part of the Antonine Wall and the fourth cohort of Gaulish Auxiliaries was stationed here. Turn left up Cochno Road just before the Golden Hill Pub. Cochno Road was known as Tarry Road as the houses used to be coated with a tar-like substance. In Cochno Road go under three sets of pylons then, directly after this, where the road bends to the right, go straight ahead on the rough road. Go through a gate and past a farm on the left. At the next farm continue straight ahead, keeping the ruined building on your right. Then bear round to the right into the valley of the Loch Humphrey Burn. Continue, keeping the burn on your left. About 200 metres up here there is a waterfall.

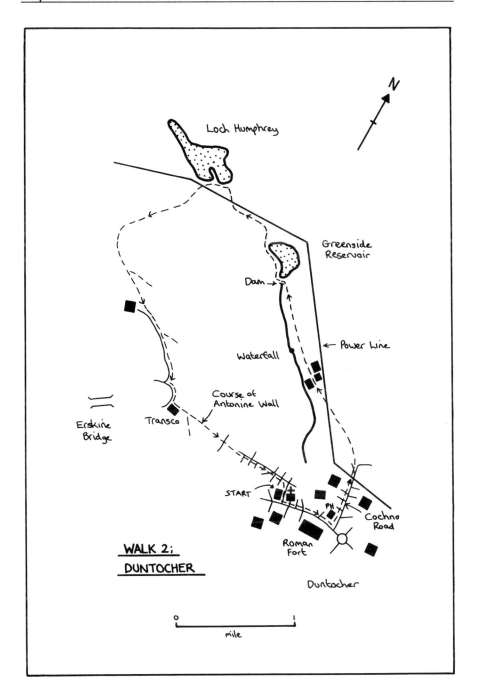

Loch Humphrey

Greenside
Reservoir

Dam →

← Power Line

Waterfall

Course of
Antonine Wall

Transco

Erskine
Bridge

START

PH

Cochno
Road

Roman
Fort

WALK 2;
DUNTOCHER

Duntocher

0
mile

Stay on this road for the next mile or so until you reach the dam of the Greenside Reservoir. Turn left across the footbridge and cross the dam. Go up a couple of metres and turn right onto a well-trodden and obvious footpath. Follow this around the south side of the reservoir. Take care as it is a steep, although not precipitous, slope on the right. At the westernmost end of the reservoir, where the burn comes in, this footpath disappears.

Cross the burn and go uphill to the lower of two sets of pylons. Turn left and walk under or just beside these pylons. After about 300 metres a clearly defined earth footpath appears. Follow this as it bends around to the right where the pylons swing left across the valley. This brings you out at a surfaced road at Loch Humphrey Reservoir. Turn left along this.

Keep on this road for the next two miles, ignoring tracks coming on and going off on both sides. As you descend you have magnificent views over the Clyde. The road crosses the valley and swings left to give panoramic views of the Erskine Bridge.

This is a cable stayed girder bridge with a total length of 1333 metres. It was opened in 1971 by HRH the Princess Royal. It is built to withstand wind speeds of as much as 130mph. It is 55 metres above the water at the highest of tides. Despite this it was closed for a while in the mid-1990s after being struck by an oil rig being towed downstream from the shipyards.

When this track joins a tarmac road coming in from a farm on the right, just keep straight on downhill on the tarmac road. At the T-junction at the bottom of the hill turn left. When you reach Old Kilpatrick Transco Station on your right, go through the farm gate on the left. Walk up the farm track, with the hedge on your right. This farm track and the next one follow the course of the Antonine Wall, which had its western terminus near here at Old Kilpatrick.

About 200 metres from the pumping station another farm track bears off to the left, follow this. This leads to a gate which you go through to follow the green lane directly ahead. At the end of the green lane, cross the metalled road to the obvious footpath in front of you and follow it to its end. Then go straight ahead up the street with houses. After about 300 metres turn right into Chapel Street – the prominent steeple is an obvious landmark. A short distance down here on your right is the car park of the Duntiglennan Inn.

It is no coincidence that this pub and the two other pubs in Duntocher have an Irish feel to them: St Patrick was captured here by pirates and taken as a slave to Ireland.

3. The Whangie

Route: Carbeth – Burncrooks – The Whangie – Queen's View

Distance: 5 miles

Map: OS Landranger 64, Glasgow

Start: Carbeth Inn, Carbeth

Access: The Whangie is a popular destination for Glaswegians at weekends. It is 10 miles north-north-west of Glasgow. As bus services are poor, it is best accessed by car. Leave Glasgow by the A82, Great Western Road. At Anniesland Cross go right onto the A739 (switchback). When this splits take the left-hand fork, the A809 for Drymen, bypassing the A81 for Milngavie. About 5 miles beyond the fork you will see a sign informing you that you are entering Stirlingshire. The Carbeth Inn is about half a mile after this on your right. There is a parking bay opposite the Carbeth Inn on the left-hand side of the road. However, this could entail reversing onto the main road to exit. So it is probably better to turn right into the Carbeth Inn's car park, which has lots of space. By bus: there is an infrequent bus service from Glasgow Buchanan Street. This stops at the Carbeth Inn. Telephone Midland Bluebird Busline on 01324 613 777 or collect a timetable at the bus station.

Carbeth Inn

There has been an inn here, serving the needs of Highlanders on their way to Glasgow, for at least 300 years. It was a coaching inn and the mail coach changed horses here. Previously it was known as the Halfway Hotel as it was halfway between Glasgow and Drymen. Carbeth means 'castle of the birches'.

Sir Walter Scott set a scene of *Rob Roy* here. Bailie Nicol Jarvie and Francis Osbaldistone sat down to a meal of broiled moor game, ewe's milk cheese, dried salmon and oaten bread washed down with excellent cognac. More recently, a few years ago some workmen turned up to remove the nuclear attack siren from here. The landlord did not even know it was there let alone where it was. They found it eventually and there is a framed newspaper clipping about the incident in the bar.

Landlord Brian Mcdade and his staff still offer hearty Highland hospitality to all, especially walkers. When I was there a two-course lunch was on offer for under £5. There is an extensive range of high quality food. It is all fresh local produce and home cooked. There is a dining room as well as a lounge and bar. Food is served in summer from Monday to Saturday 12.00 to 19.45, and on Sundays 12.30 to 19.45.

The bar is dark wood, and the floors are of stone or flagged. The decor is mainly of Belhaven 80/- barrels. The real ales are Belhaven 80/- (there's a surprise) and St Andrew's ale. The bar also has old mirrors, and pictures of the area and the inn in times past. A wood-fired metal stove heats the bar and supplies hot water. There are fruit machines and a cigarette machine. Opening hours are Monday to Thursday 12.00 to 23.00, Friday and Saturday 12.00 to 24.00 and Sunday 12.30 to 23.00. Keg products include Guinness, Belhaven Best, Tennents Lager and Dry Blackthorn Cider. No children are allowed in the bar after 17.00. Dogs must be supervised at all times. A board gives the OG and ABV of the ales on offer. The lounge is carpeted and has hunting scenes on the walls as well as old advertising posters. The dining room is walled in stone and has an extensive wine list. A beer garden outside gives views over the surrounding hills. Telephone 01360 770002.

The Whangie

This geological oddity on Auchineden Hill has long been a popular day trip for Glaswegians. It also attracts climbers and geologists. The name 'Whangie' describes it well. A 'whangie' is a Scottish word for a slice. It looks as if some giant hand has taken a knife to the cliff face and sliced some off. You can walk between the cliff and the slice. It is approximately 100 metres long, 20 metres deep and one metre wide. This immense fissure is in one of the plugs of lava that block the old volcanic caldera of the Kilpatrick Hills.

Local legend says that Auld Nick, having attended a coven in the Campsies, was on his way to another in Dumbarton. As he bypassed this cliff, being in good form and fettle, he flicked his tail at it and so made The Whangie. One theory for its formation is that the softer red sandstone around was eroded and undermined the cliff so that it split. Another theory is that it was caused by glacial plucking when, at the end of the last Ice Age, the glaciers retreated and pulled the front of the rock face away.

When Highlanders went reiving cattle in the fertile lowlands of Lennox nearby they used to hide their stolen cattle in nooks and crannies of The Whangie. After the 1745 rebellion, Jacobites hid here from Cumberland's butchers. The Whangie and 196 hectares (492 acres) of land surrounding it are now the property of the National Trust for Scotland.

The Walk

Come out of the Carbeth Inn, turn left down the road and proceed for about 100 metres. Go right through a kissing gate that is on the right-hand side of a farm gate between two stone walls. Walk up the beaten earth and gravel cart track. After a couple of hundred metres, go through another gate and continue up this road. Go through yet another gate to stay on this road. Bypass the road to Auchineden Farm on your

The Whangie

right, and cross a ladder stile to the left of a gate. Cross another ladder stile to the right of a gate.

When you reach the isolated house turn right, ignoring the track on your left to the barn. Go through a gate to the left of the house and follow the road on. Bear right with the road and into a forest. About half a mile past the house you come to a four-way junction. Turn left up the tarmac road here. Walk up past Burncrooks Water Treatment Plant on your right. Go over the stile to the left of the gate here and stay on this road for about three-quarters of a mile, going past two tracks on the left. As the forest ends on your left and the reservoir begins, look for a green path on your right going off at ninety degrees. At this point there are two blank notice boards beside the road and a stile on your left.

Follow this wide and obvious path uphill through the heather. The Whangie is about three-quarters of a mile along this path. At the top of the hill it comes into sight. It is the pinnacle of riven rock at the far end of the crags on your right. This path splits along here but rejoins later so take either. Just before The Whangie you come to a T-junction with an extremely good path. The Local Authority, in conjunction with Scottish Natural Heritage, has recently employed a firm of professional path makers to lay it.

Your path is left, but if you like you can divert right and up to the Trig Point on top of The Whangie for an even more spectacular view. Having gone left at the path T-junction, you then pick your way among the rocks at the bottom of The Whangie, which looms above and to the right of you. Pick up the path at the far end of the boulders. This leads to Queen's View, about a mile away. From here there are spectacular views over Loch Lomond and the Southern Highlands. Contour along and gently down the hillside until you reach a ladder stile. Cross this and descend more steeply to the car park at Queen's View. On this path you will see numerous meadow pipits. These belong to the 'wbb' family: wee brown birds! They are identifiable as they fly away from you by the longitudinal white stripes along the outer edges of their tails.

Queen's View was named for Queen Victoria. As part of the restoration work the car park and viewing point have recently been improved. Turn right down the main road here. After about 100 metres turn right where it is signed for 'Courtyard and Auchineden House'. Walk up through the narrow belt of trees. About 200 metres up here go over a ladder stile on your left and along the track beyond it. Please keep strictly to the track as this is a wildlife conservation area. After about half a mile on this track, climb over a huge ladder stile and turn left along the tarmac road. Walk up to the main road and turn right. Walk alongside the main road for about 300 metres. There is a good fenced path for much of this distance. Once under the pylons and past the junction the Carbeth Inn is on your left. When I was walking along here a rabbit pursued by a dog came running up towards me – talk about being between the Devil and the deep blue sea! It escaped into a field.

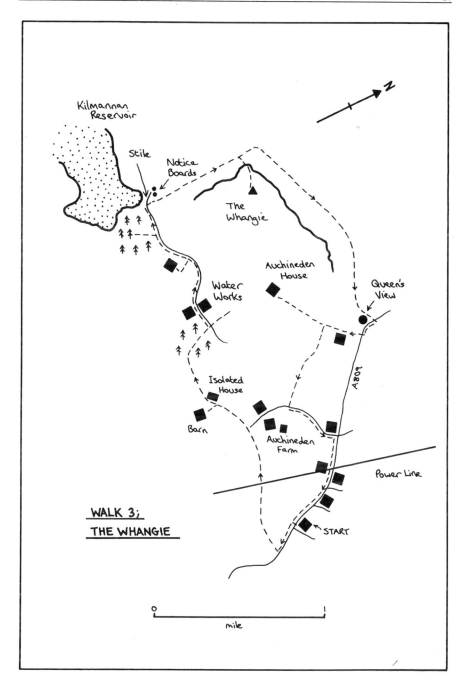

Kilmannan Reservoir

Stile

Notice Boards

The Whangie

Auchineden House

Queen's View

Water Works

A809

Isolated House

Barn

Auchineden Farm

Power Line

START

WALK 3;
THE WHANGIE

0   1
mile

4. Buchlyvie

Route: Buchlyvie – Flanders Moss – River Forth – Over Easter Offerance – Gartentruach – Easter Mye – Wester Mye

Distance: 7 miles

Map: OS Landranger 57, Stirling and The Trossachs

Start: Village Inn, Buchlyvie

Access: Buchlyvie is about 20 miles north of Glasgow city centre. By car: take the A81 for Aberfoyle out of Glasgow. Go through Strathblane/Blanefield. About half a mile beyond the white-painted Glengoyne Distillery on your right, take the A875 for Killearn and Balfron, also on your right. About two miles after Balfron you arrive at a T-junction with the A811. Turn right along here, signposted for Stirling. About two miles further on you come to Buchlyvie. The Village Inn is at the far end of the village on your left. There is no car park but parking is unrestricted here. Possibly your best bet for parking here is the large lay-by 50 metres beyond the Village Inn and on the same side of the road. By bus: The Village Inn is on the bus route from Glasgow to Stirling via Balfron. The bus passes the pub door so ask to be put off there. The service, however, is sparse. For information telephone Midland Bluebird Busline on 01324 613 777.

The Village Inn

This is an old inn and one of the oldest buildings in the village. The locals tell me that it was here when Sir Walter Scott visited Buchlyvie and sat in a seat above the village, looking out over the Highlands and gaining inspiration for his works. However, there is no record of him having a drink here. In those days the pub was called the Red Lion. You will see a small red lion on the wall outside.

The first historical record I can find of it is in 1876. It was then that the councillors and JPs of Buchlyvie gathered here to choose a new provost. Mr John Graham was selected as the right person to fill the office with decorum and gravitas. Subsequently, it became a popular stop with cyclists and offered special rates to members of the Scottish Cyclists' Union.

Current landlord Johnnie Simpson still offers handsome hospitality, but I could not manage to arrange special rates for walkers. However, there is a beer garden with stunning views over the Highlands. The pleasantly furbished restaurant also shares this view. The bar is attractively decorated and features hats and brass. There are free local newspapers and pictures of old Buchlyvie.

The cellar is too warm for real ale. On draught are Strongbow Dry Cider, Tartan Special, John Smiths Best, McEwans 70/-, Guinness, McEwans Lager, Miller, Becks, Budweiser and Holstein Pils. Opening hours are 11.00 to 24.00 Monday to Thursday, 11.00 to 01.00 Friday and Saturday and 12.30 to 24.00 on Sundays. There are fruit machines and a television in the bar. Some nights there is folk music with local musicians.

There is a good selection of food with choices of dips or salad dressings. The vegetarian choice includes vegetarian haggis. Desserts and coffee are available. There is a good wine list. There is a children's menu and high chairs are supplied if necessary. Food is served 12.00 to 21.00 Monday to Saturday and 12.30 to 21.00 on Sundays. Telephone 01360 850 383.

The inn at Buchlyvie

Flanders Moss

This used to be a quaking bog covered with peat up to four metres thick. Only a few Highland caterans (rustlers) and smugglers could pick their way through this on submerged causeways. Mountains and the sea blocked access to the West of Scotland, the Forth Estuary denied entry to the east and Flanders Moss was an impassable obstacle in the centre. Consequently, large invading armies had to go through a narrow neck of land between Flanders Moss and the Forth Estuary where the river could be crossed. This is why some of the major battles of the Wars of Independence took place here, such as Stirling Brig and Bannockburn.

The nature of Flanders Moss remained like this until 1766. Lord Kames of Blairdrummond, a Law Lord, inherited 2000 acres of land in this area, of which only a tenth was cultivable, arable land. He hit on the idea of using Highlanders cleared off their ancestral lands by greedy aristocrats to clear this land for him. Highland Clearances becoming Highland Clearers, ironic eh?

Lord Kames offered these dispossessed people rent-free crofts for a limited period. He also offered them enough oatmeal to eat while they cleared the land and established crops. The Highlanders, finding that conventional cottages would not stand up on the quaking peat, dug into the moss to make houses of peat. Lord Kames gave them timber for their roofs and they covered the timbers with heather. These houses were snug and dry. The locals sarcastically called the Highlanders 'Moss Lairds', as they were afraid of them. But the canny Highlanders sold the peat that they cleared to nearby towns such as Stirling as fuel. And, by much hard work and ingenuity they carved out fertile farms from the Moss and became Moss Lairds indeed, respected members of the local community.

The Walk

Turn right out of the Village Inn and go along the main road for about 100 metres in the direction of the clock tower. At Buchlyvie Licensed Grocer's turn right onto the B835 (Station Road). Go down the road and across a bridge spanning a burn. About 100 metres beyond the bridge turn right into a farm road, just at the Buchlyvie signpost. Walk down this farm road for about 100 metres, going past a house on the left and under a bridge. Immediately under this bridge turn right and scramble up to the disused railway line path. At the top of the little path to the dis-

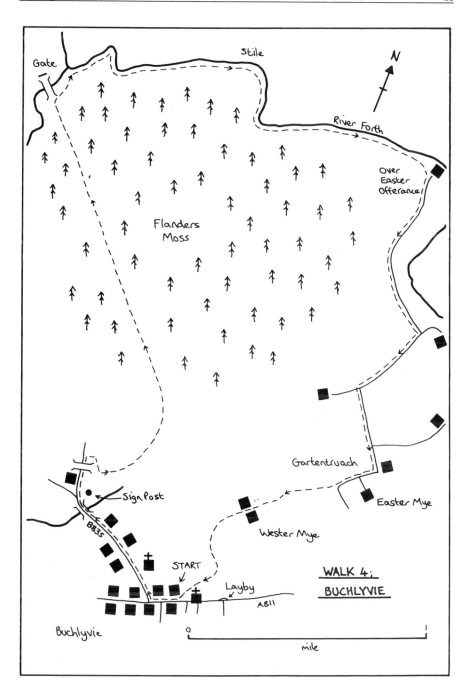

Gate

Stile

N

River Forth

Over
Easter
Offerance

Flanders
Moss

Gartentruach

Sign Post

B835

Wester Mye

Easter Mye

START

Layby

A811

WALK 4;
BUCHLYVIE

Buchlyvie

0   1

mile

used railway line, turn left along the railway path, keeping the bridge behind you.

Follow the railway line footpath along for about 100 metres and then bear left with it. This is the Aberfoyle branch line of the old railway, built by the North British Railway Company. One thing about railway line paths is that they always have gentle gradients. The path then straightens up and enters a forest. The forest is fir but the path is lined with deciduous trees so it is a pleasant walk. Walk along this path for about a mile. At the end of the forest there is a bridge over a burn with a gate at the far end of it. Turn right onto a footpath beside the burn before the bridge. Follow this well-marked footpath through sometimes-luxuriant vegetation along the burn bank for about 100 metres, until you reach the River Forth.

Turn right along the Forth and follow the footpath along its bank. The anglers here are quite friendly – unlike most anglers who never give you a civil word. Keep the Forth on your left and the forest on your right for about a mile, crossing footbridges over side streams as they appear. As the forest ends, cross a stile and continue walking beside the Forth through river meadows (very enjoyable). The footpath fades in and out but you just keep the Forth on your left. After about a mile of this you arrive at the ruined buildings of Over Easter Offerance. Walk up to the nearside of the buildings, turning right away from the Forth. Go left through the farm gate, closing it behind you. Go through the farmyard briefly and turn right onto the fenced farm road away from the river.

Go through another gate and follow the track down beside the fence on your right. Go through a further gate and continue with the river and then a fence on your left. When this track comes to a T-junction with a tarmac road, go through a gate and right along the tarmac road, away from the farm. After about 400 metres this road goes sharply left. Go with the road at this point, ignoring the farm track in front of you. There is a metal outline of a cow dangling on a telephone pole here. At Gartentruach Farm on your left, follow the road around to the right. Go past Easter Mye on your left. About 100 metres beyond Easter Mye, where the road bends sharply left, go straight ahead on the cart track. Follow this along through the farmyard at Wester Mye. Keep on this track beyond Wester Mye. This brings you out at the Village Inn in Buchlyvie. Buchlyvie has public toilets at the lay-by 50 metres to your left on the main road.

5. Kippen

Route: Kippen – Glentirranmuir – Dasher – Cauldhame – Arngomery – Old Smiddy

Distance: 5½ miles

Map: OS Landranger 57, Stirling and the Trossachs

Start: Cross Keys, Kippen.

Access: Kippen is about 25 miles north-east of Glasgow. By car: take the A81 out of Glasgow. Go through Strathblane/Blanefield. About half a mile beyond the white-painted Glengoyne Distillery on your right, take the A875 for Killearn and Balfron, also on your right. About two miles after Balfron you arrive at a T-junction with the A811. Turn right here, signposted for Stirling. Go through Buchlyvie and Arnprior. About a mile beyond Arnprior you will see a green sign followed by two blue ones guiding you right on the B8037 for Kippen. Follow this road for about two miles, ignoring a B road off signposted for Kippen. At Kippen Cross the road sign points left to Callender and right to Fintry, both on the B822. Go right here. The Cross Keys is about 50 metres up on your right. There is a parking bay with room for seven or eight cars directly in front of the pub. If these are full, park in the street. Parking is unrestricted and the locals are tolerant according to mine host at the Cross Keys. By bus: the Glasgow to Stirling via Balfron service has a stop at Kippen Cross, but this is not a frequent service. For details call Midland Bluebird Busline on 01324 613 777 or pick up a timetable at the Travel Centre, St Enoch's Square, Glasgow.

Cross Keys

When you walk into this pub you may experience a sense of déjà vu. You may not have been here before, but you may well have seen it before. A number of scenes from *Monty Python and the Holy Grail* were shot here. In fact, they still have the original clapperboard behind the bar, which they will show you if you ask. The building dates back to 1703. Later two houses were knocked together to make a pub. This was a pub from at least the early 19th century, when it offered a gill of whisky with cakes and cheese for the princely sum of 3d. A previous

The Monty Python clapperboard

owner of the inn was a key manufacturer and as it is in close proximity to Kippen Cross it was called the Cross Keys.

Mr and Mrs Watt run a pub that only a string of superlatives can describe. It is recommended both in the 1997 Egon Ronay guide for food and accommodation and in the *Which* guide to country pubs. It is in the AA book of Britain's best pubs. Manageress Mandy Dow gained the Employee of the Year award from the Scottish Licensed Trade Association in 1996. And it has recently been voted the best place to eat out by tourists in the Loch Lomond, Stirlingshire and Trossachs area.

The lounge is that of a lovely, old-fashioned pub: all dark wood beams and light plaster work with exposed stone around the fire. The public bar is in the same mould. They also have a restaurant, The Vine, which has the story of the Kippen Vine in pictures on its walls. The food, of course, is excellent. It is possible to have a real Scottish three-course meal of broth, stovies and home-made clootie dumpling. There is a limited vegetarian choice. They offer reduced price smaller portions for OAPs and children. There is a children's play area. Food is served on weekdays 12.00 to 14.00 and 17.30 to 21.30. On Saturdays it is 12.00 to 14.00 and 17.15 to 21.30, and on Sundays 12.30 to 14.00 and

17.15 to 21.30. If you are coming outside these hours in the day and with a party of 15 or more they will be happy to supply food for you if you phone in advance.

The real ale is Broughtons Greenmantle. Other pumps have Strongbow Dry Cider, Guinness, Gilliespies Malt Stout, Tartan Special, McEwans 70/-, John Smiths and Miller Pilsner. Opening hours are Monday to Friday 12.00 to 14.30 and 17.30 to 23.30 (Fridays 24.30). On Saturdays 12.00 to 14.30 and 17.15 to 23.30, and Sundays 12.30 to 23.30. There is also a beer garden.

They are delighted to accommodate walkers and have a free leaflet giving details of walks around Kippen. If you wanted to stay here, say for a weekend, the Kippen area has many good, well-marked paths. Telephone 01786 870 293.

Kippen

This is an extremely picturesque old village with many interesting buildings. The gable and belfry of a church built in 1691 are part of the current church. The bell, which is labelled 1618, comes from an even earlier church. The Black Bull used to be the main pub in the village and is now a restored National Trust property. This dates from 1729 and still has its twelve-paned glass windows and scrolled skewputs on its gables. The Old Smiddy is also a National Trust property. Andrew Rennie was the last of his family to work here and remained until his death at 97 in 1985. The Rennies started the Smiddy in Kippen in 1721. This property is not open to the public at the moment. I was told in the village that the National Trust cannot get anyone to run it. To find out if it is open and for details of the Black Bull, ring the National Trust for Scotland on 0131 243 9555.

Kippen was once a kingdom. James V was staying at Stirling and sent his men out to catch a deer. They caught one near Kippen, but the local laird, John Buchanan, and his men took it from them. When they protested that it was for the king, John Buchanan retorted that he was King of Kippen. James V, more intrigued than annoyed by this, rode over to meet John Buchanan. The two got on famously so John Buchanan was allowed to call himself King of Kippen.

Less friendly was the visit of Rob Roy. As he was going past Kippen with a herd of stolen cattle he was attacked by dragoons. He drove the soldiers off but, incensed with the pointless bloodshed, as he saw it, he stole all of Kippen's cattle as he suspected the Kippenites of complicity with the dragoons. This was the Hership (Hardship) O'Kippen.

In the 18th century, 20 or 30 young girls were employed here in tambouring. A tambour is a frame over which muslin is stretched to be embroidered. However, Kippen has always been a mainly agricultural village. Of a parish roll of 411 at the end of the 18th century, 188 were either farmers or employed on farms. The Kippen Vine was also of note agriculturally. First planted in 1891 by local market gardener Duncan Buchanan, it was producing 600 bunches a year by 1910. By 1960 it was producing 2000 bunches of grapes annually. It covered 500 square metres and stretched for more than 100 metres long. The trunk was 1.5 metres thick. This was the world's largest vine under glass and produced good quality table grapes of the Gros Coleman variety. It was destroyed in 1964 as cheap imports made it uneconomic. These days it would be preserved as a tourist attraction.

The famous Glasgow architect Alexander (Greek) Thompson was born in Kippen.

One black mark for Kippen. Its promotional literature states that its public toilets are open 24 hours a day, 7 days a week. They were locked and barred when I was there.

The Walk

As you come out of the Cross Keys turn left down Main Street. About 50 metres down here turn right opposite the War memorial to go along Burnside. Climb gently out of the village on this quiet road, pausing to enjoy extensive views over the Forth Valley and Southern Highlands to your left. On a clear day you can see the Wallace Monument near Stirling on your left front. Proceed along the road, bypassing roads to left and right.

At the end of the road go directly ahead through the yard and onto the track on the other side. Follow this track through the woods, it degrades into a footpath. At the end of the wood go through the kissing gate. Follow the cart track in front of you, with the fence on your close right. This takes you across a burn via a bridge. Once across the bridge turn immediately right through a gate and go up a footpath with the burn on your right.

At the end of the footpath, straight ahead of you, are the cliffs of the Gargunnock Hills. You can see why one of them is called Black Craig.

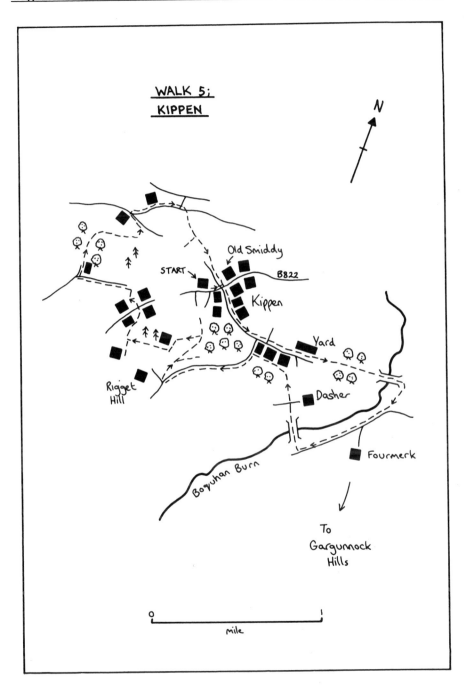

WALK 5;
KIPPEN

N

Old Smiddy

START

B822

Kippen

Yard

Rigget
Hill

Dasher

Boquhan Burn

Fourmerk

To
Gargunnock
Hills

0   1

mile

Turn right along the minor tarmac road here. On your left you will pass the entrance to Fourmerk Highlanders Stud. There are lots of picturesque Highland cattle here. Keep on this road with the burn on your right.

About 150 metres after the forest ends on your right, go through a farm gate on the right, closing it behind you. Then go down the sunken track to the bridge over the burn. At the gate on the bridge go to the right of it, there is a gap. Go directly onwards on this track uphill and through a gate. Cross a track leading to/from Dasher Farm and continue uphill. Keep with this track down the other side of the hill as it bends left with the fence on your near right. As the track enters woodland, look to your right for a stile in the furthermost corner of the field. Cross this and walk down the path to the minor road. There is a footpath sign here pointing back the way you have come.

Turn left up the minor road. You may hear a lot of banging here as there is a clay pigeon shoot on the hill above you. There is a seat here if you want a rest. Near the top of the gentle slope there is a road (Rigget Hill) going off to the right. Look right again and you will see a footpath going half-backwards through the wood. Follow this down. It is slightly confusing as another path shortly branches off this. However, if you follow the steps built into the path you will not go astray.

Come out of the wood by a little footbridge and wander down a path between trees on one side and fields on the other. Walk across the left-hand edge of the playing fields until you come to a minor road/cart track. Turn left up this. After about 200 metres, just before the house gates, there is a public footpath sign on your left. Follow this along the side of the pinewood. At the end of the wood go through a semi-kissing gate immediately in front of you. Then cross a footbridge and turn right at its end, at the public footpath sign.

At the end of the footpath go directly ahead on the semi-tarmac track. This leads to a T-junction with a minor tarmac road. Turn right here at a sign for Mid Redgate Hill. At the junction at the end of this minor road, go straight across the B822 and onto the track between the houses. Follow this left and right as it leads you to another tarmac road. The cone-shaped mountain framed in front of you as you walk down this track is Ben Ledi (2855ft/879m). It does not sound a lot, but if you have slogged up it you will know differently.

As you turn left along this tarmac road you may see a selection of exotic hens on your left. Where the road forks go right, keeping the burn on your left. When the road ends go past a house on your right and proceed down the footpath in front of you. Next go through a kissing gate and follow the track through a field and away from the burn on your left. There are some majestic old firs along here. When this farm track meets a semi-tarmac road, go straight ahead then follow this around to the left to a T-junction with a metalled road.

Cross the metalled road to the pavement and turn left along it for about 100 metres. A metalled road then doubles back to your right. Go along this, ignoring the 'Road Closed'sign: it does not apply to you. When this road bears left to the main road, go diagonally right up a cart track. At the end of the cart track go onto the semi-tarmac road directly in front of you. When this forks at some houses bear left. Ignore another road on your right and keep on frontward. Eventually, a walk up cobbles brings you to the Old Smiddy at the start of this Rennies Loan. Turn right past the War memorial to reach the Cross Keys.

6. Aberfoyle

Route: Covenanters Inn – Lochlan Spling – Gartnaul – Garbeg Hill

Distance: 5 miles

Map: OS Landranger 57, Stirling and the Trossachs area

Start: Covenanters Inn, Kirkton of Aberfoyle

Access: Aberfoyle is 30 miles north of Glasgow in the Trossachs area. Access is best by car as the bus service is infrequent. By car: from Glasgow city centre take the A82 westwards towards Loch Lomond. At Anniesland Cross go right onto the A739 (Switchback). About two miles down here, before Bearsden Cross, take the A81 to the right and follow this almost to Aberfoyle. The A81 is variously signposted to Milngavie, Strathblane or Aberfoyle. Just before you reach the hills turn left on the A821, signposted for Aberfoyle. Go through the village. At the far end of the village the A821 turns sharply right. Go directly ahead. Ten metres past the junction turn left down Manse Road. Go over the narrow bridge and 100 metres down this road take a right, as directed by the Covenanters Inn signboard. About 200 metres up this road a signpost directs you right into the entry of the Covenanters Inn. The first entrance is the exit from the pub. There is a fair amount of car parking at the inn. By bus: there is a service at widely spaced intervals from Glasgow Buchanan Street Bus Station. Telephone Midland Bluebird Busline on 01324 613777.

The Covenanters Inn

This is a very interesting place. Although it is not very old, it has an interesting history. At the end of the 19th century two houses were built here. In 1935 one of them became the Inchrie Hotel. The two buildings were subsequently joined together to make the present-day hotel.

In April 1949 a Glasgow lawyer, Dr John McCormick, chaired a two-day conference here from which came the Second Covenant. This bound the signatories to try for a Scottish parliament. It was first signed by the Duke of Montrose, and afterwards by two million of Scotland's population. The inn was then renamed The Covenanters.

When the Stone of Destiny was stolen from Westminster Abbey (or rightfully reclaimed as one might say) in 1953, it was hidden under the stairs of the Covenanters Inn. The walls of the bar have framed copies of newspaper clippings about this. These give a period flavour if you also read the other news stories and adverts. There are also newspaper clippings on the wall about pony trekking being started here in 1954. This was the first place in Scotland to do this.

The Covenanters Inn looks a lot older than it is as it has many bits of older houses such as old fireplaces, with real fires in the winter, incorporated into it. Despite this it is very snug and comfortable. The bar is one of nooks and crannies, including an interesting library with books and magazines. As you come through the impressive stone and wood entrance there is a relief map of the area.

There is no real ale on draught but pint bottles of real ales such as Heather Ale and Broughton Breweries'products are available. Keg beers include Tartan Special and Gillespies Malt Stout. Scrumpy Jack is also on draught. The bar is open 11.00 to 24.00 seven days a week.

Bar meals are available from 12.00 to 14.00 and 18.00 to 20.30 seven days a week. All the food is fresh and local produce is used wherever possible. There is local haggis and Aberfoyle sausage. The soup and

The Covenanters Inn

pâté are home made and all the cheeses in the ploughman's are Scottish. This pub attracts lots of ramblers so they are used to walkers. If you want food outside normal serving hours and you are a party of ten or more, then if you phone them a week in advance they will be happy to lay something on for you. Telephone 01877 382 347.

Aberfoyle

In 1691 the Reverend Robert Kirk of Aberfoyle published a book, *The Secret Commonwealth*, on elves and fairies. In 1692 he disappeared while walking over Doon Hill near Aberfoyle. In revenge for revealing their secrets, the fairies are supposed to have trapped him in torment in the trunk of a twisted Scots Pine on the top of Doon Hill.

In the early 1700s Rob Roy was frequently in the area: the ancestral MacGregor lands are at Glengyle at the head of Loch Katrine and at Inversnaid on eastern Loch Lomond. He was a decent man driven to crime by bankruptcy, yet he never fully gave in to banditry. He was always willing to help redress wrongs and he also helped the poor. He was a kind of Scottish Robin Hood. He invented the concept of protection money. 'Pay me a small sum annually and I will not rustle your cattle.'

The most famous scene in the novel *Rob Roy* took place at the Clachan of Aberfoyle, which was a mile outside Aberfoyle on the B829 to Stronlachar. In this scene Bailie Nicol Jarvie defends himself with a red-hot coulter (plough blade) being used as a poker. The Bailie Nicol Jarvie Hotel used to have the 'original' hanging on a tree outside it. Unfortunately, this establishment is now closed.

The Trossachs

In Gaelic this means 'the bristling country', and bristle it does with trees and rocky promontories. The Trossachs were originally the small area between Loch Katrine and Loch Achray. However, nowadays the name encompasses the region between eastern Loch Lomond and Callendar. The area was first made famous by Sir Walter Scott's poem 'The Lady of the Lake' published in 1810. Its publicity was further boosted by Scott's novel *Rob Roy* in 1817. Much of the action in this book takes place in the Trossachs.

Perhaps the attraction of the Trossachs is that they are to the Highlands what Bonsai are to trees. It is also a fairly compact area which is easily accessible from the populous and civilised central belt of Scotland. Whatever the reason for their attraction, they have inspired many artists of various disciplines. Coleridge, Dorothy and William Wordworth, John Ruskin and James Hogg 'the Ettrick Shepherd' were inspired by the area and Millais painted here.

The Walk

As this is a forest walk and these are notoriously difficult to navigate I have given you a waymarked walk. However, I have also given you directions as waymarking can be altered or removed. All you have to do is follow the blue waymarkers, but if you are wise you will check that these conform to the directions I have taken the trouble to give you. This could be a good walk for when there is snow on the ground obscuring footpaths as this walk is exclusively on forest tracks that it would take many feet of snow to hide.

Leave the Covenanters Inn by the entrance through which you arrived. Turn right up the tarmac road. Pick up your first blue waymarker just after the 'No Unauthorised Vehicles' sign. About a quarter of a mile up here on your right there is a rowan tree with the silver bark of a birch. Walk about another half a mile beyond this and a waymarker guides you right on a forest track. There is a damaged metal post here and another forest track on the left about 20 metres past your turn. This is Queen Elizabeth Forest Park, 20,000 hectares (50,000 acres) commemorating Queen Elizabeth II's accession to the throne in 1952.

This track bears left and goes past Lochan Spling on your left (a lochan is a small loch). After about half a mile it fades right and gently uphill. After about another half mile you go left at a T-junction. This is not waymarked until you are about 20 metres past the turn. Walk down here for about another half a mile until you reach a T-junction with a wider forest road. Here head right.

Continue along here until you arrive at the ruined cottage of Gartnaul on the right. Ahead of you here is Duchray Forest. In the Second World War about 1,750,000 tons of ammunition were stored here. Some of the dumps where it was stored are still here, but thankfully none of the ammunition. These munitions were transported by rail to Glasgow and were used by Montgomery's forces at Alamein. Your route is left uphill at the ruined cottage. This track bends left and along the contour of the hillside through a set of gates.

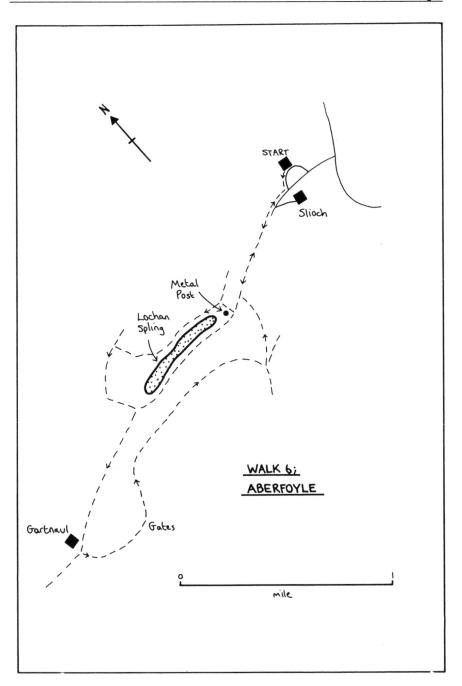

N

START

Slioch

Metal
Post

Lochan
Spling

WALK 6;
ABERFOYLE

Gartnaul   Gates

0   1
                              mile

As you walk along here, you may see some bright red rock leaching its colour into water. This will be byrites. There was an old byrites mine here that was last used over a century ago. The mineral was used as paint pigment and as a grinding paste.

After about a mile along here and some good views over the forest you reach a T-junction. Take the road to the left. About 50 metres further on you take the left fork at a junction in the track, and about 300 metres further on you turn right at the offset four-way junction. Proceed along this track, past the house called Slioch, for about three-quarters of a mile until you come to the Covenanters Inn on your left. Look out for the signs, as they face the other way.

7. Mauchline

Route: Mauchline — Ballochmyle — Haugh — Mosshead — Bogwood — Laurland — Hillhead

Distance: 6 miles

Map: OS Landranger 70, Ayr, Kilmarnock.

Start: Loudon Arms, Mauchline

Access: By bus: there is a regular direct bus service between Glasgow and Mauchline during the day but not evenings, Monday to Saturday. On Sundays it is necessary to change at Kilmarnock but it is still a regular service. For details telephone 0141 636 3195. By car: drive westwards out of Glasgow on the M8, towards Glasgow Airport. At junction 22 take the M77 for Kilmarnock. This leads directly onto the A77 (T). After about 13 miles, as you bypass Kilmarnock, you will see the A76 (T) on your left, signposted for Mauchline. About eight miles down here you arrive in Mauchline. At the bottom of the hill in Mauchline, go right at the traffic lights on the B743 for Ayr. About 100 metres along here turn right into the free public car park signposted on your right. This is immediately before the Loudon Arms, which is also on the right.

Loudon Arms Hotel

There has been a pub on this site since at least 1780. Previous pubs here were old coaching inns. It is the home of the Loudon Spout, Ayrshire's oldest artesian well. This can be seen spouting (surprise, surprise) outside the pub. Horses used to be watered from an old stone trough beneath this and local people took domestic water from the tap. There are pictures of this in the lounge. The well has been here since at least the turn of the century. Mauchline means 'hill of wells'.

In 1786 this was John MacClelland's Inn, where worthies and drouthies ('drouthy' means 'thirsty') met. Robert Burns regularly attended a reading class in the inn that year. The pub was part of Gavin Hamilton's estate. Gavin Hamilton was a friend of Robert Burns and the lawyer who formally married him to Jean Armour. Eric Caldow, the ex-Rangers and Scotland full-back, also drinks here.

There used to be a quoiting green out the back. This was a very popular pastime. The miners pitched quoits at targets. There are a couple of quoits on the windowsill of the bar. Heft them in your hand, the players must have been built like blacksmiths. The curling stone in the bar was made in Mauchline. The only curling stone manufacturer in the world is in Mauchline. The stone is made of Ailsa Craig granite.

Alan and Barbara Brighton run an unpretentious, friendly village pub, where all are offered cheerful hospitality – including walkers. In the bar there are pictures of Burns and Burns scenes, as you might expect. A real fire's flames flicker in winter. The lounge has leatherette banquettes, pictures of old Mauchline, dark wood beams, old washboards and stoneware bottles. It is old-world but comfortable and welcoming. A copy of the Declaration of Arbroath hangs on the wall. There are also darts, fruit machines and a pool table.

Talking of tables, good home-made food is served from Thursday to Sunday 12.00 to 15.00 and 17.00 to 20.30. There is always a real ale but it is a guest not a resident. It was Belhaven Jaggy Bunnet when I was there. Keg beers include Belhaven Best and Light, Tartan Special, Carlsberg Lager, Tennents Lager and Guinness. There is also Strongbow Cider on draught. Opening hours are Monday to Thursday 11.00 to 24.00, Friday and Saturday 11.00 to 01.00, and Sunday 11.30 to 24.00. Telephone 01290 551011.

Robert Burns

Robert Burns was born in Alloway, just south of Ayr, in 1759. In 1777 his family moved to Lochlea Farm near Tarbolton in central Ayrshire. The family were poor tenant farmers but tried hard to educate themselves. In 1780 Burns, his brother Gilbert and five other local lads formed the Bachelors' Club in Tarbolton to debate issues of interest to them. In 1781 he became a freemason in Tarbolton. One of his fellow lodge members was Mauchline lawyer Gavin Hamilton, who became a friend and mentor of Burns.

In 1781/2 Burns tried to establish a heckling business (flax dressing) in Irvine, but it failed. In 1784 the family moved to farm at Mossgiel near Mauchline. The factor letting the farm was Gavin Hamilton. Burns' first illegitimate child was born to a local girl, Lizzy Paton, in 1785. This inspired 'A Poet's Welcome to his Love-Begotten Daughter'. In Mauchline he wrote 'Death and Dr Hornbrook' after a Masonic lodge quarrel with Tarbolton dominie John Wilson. He also wrote 'Holy Willie's Prayer', in support of Gavin Hamilton who was embroiled in a doctrinal dispute with the Kirk. In 1786 he met Jean Armour. When she became pregnant her parents sent her away and rejected Burns, despite them having gone through a form of marriage. Burns thought that Jean had rejected him. In 1786 he planned to go to Jamaica to work as a bookkeeper but in this year he met Highland Mary and became engaged to her. She died of a fever in Greenock while returning to him from her family home in Dunoon.

The need for emigration was removed by the success of the *Kilmarnock Edition* of his poems. This included 'To A Mouse', 'The Cotters' Saturday Night' and 'Holy Willie's Prayer'. He was lionised by Edinburgh society and taken up by a powerful patron, the 14th Earl of Glencairn. In 1787 the second edition was published, including the address to a haggis. He then returned home a hero and resumed with Jean Armour. In 1788 Gavin Hamilton married him to Jean Armour. By this time she had had a second set of twins by him. She also fostered one of his numerous illegitimate progeny. He then went to farm at Ellisland in Dumfriesshire as he was never happy earning his living only by his pen. He wrote 'Tam O'Shanter' in 1791 and he also wrote 'Auld Lang Syne' at Ellisland.

In 1791 he moved into Dumfries town to work as an exciseman. 'Scots Wha Hae' was published in 1793. He died of endocarditis in 1796. This was caused by rheumatic fever which he caught when he was younger, when he was also overworked and underfed. He did not die of drink. He wrote about drink but by the standards of his day and as reported by his contemporaries, Burns was not a heavy drinker. In fact, to quote the words of the caretaker/guide at the Bachelors' Club, 'When you consider the volume of his work, Burns was not an alcoholic but a workaholic.'

The Walk

Turn left out of the Loudon Arms and left again into the car park. At the far right corner of the car park follow the brick-surfaced footpath between walls. Take the right-hand fork up here and go past Mauchline Parish Church on your right. This is signposted for Burns House. This takes you past Auld Nanse Tinnock's on the right and Burns House on the left. Nanse Tinnock was a village alewife in whose hostelry Burns drank. Burns House was not open when I was there but you may be luckier.

At the end of Castle Street go straight across Mauchline Cross (the traffic lights) into High Street. This is marked the B743 for Sorn. About 100 metres up here dog-leg back and right into Mansefield Road. Keep on this road. Continue when it becomes an unmade road. After about 300 metres of farm track, just before it goes into Walton Farm, turn right on another unmade road. Walk down here for about 200 metres. When you reach the tarmac of the B705 turn left along this. Approximately 100 metres along here, where the road bends sharply left, take the minor road on the right at the chevrons.

When you arrive at the A76 (T) go left, signposted for Dumfries, Auchinleck and Cumnock. Walk down here for about 300 metres, there are cycle tracks on both sides of the road that you can walk in. At the end of the wood on your right turn right onto a minor road between white posts. About 50 metres down here go right at the fork; the Ballochmyle Viaduct is now in sight ahead of you. This viaduct was used in filming the *Mission Impossible* film. After another 100 metres, as the road bears left there is a stile on your right. Once across the stile go down the obvious grassy path ahead to the woods. Here cross another stile and follow the path left through the woods. About 50 metres in take the right-hand path at a fork. Cross a footbridge and continue on this path along the valley side and under the viaduct. Take the second path on the left after the viaduct.

This is the highest railway bridge in the UK at 167ft (51.5 metres). When it was built it was the world's longest single span stone viaduct – about 180ft (55 metres) across. It was built between 1846 and 1848 by 400 navvies and took a year and seven months to complete. It was built by the Glasgow, Paisley, Kilmarnock and Ayr Rail Company. It carries the Kilmarnock to Dumfries line.

Walk beside the River Ayr for approximately 600 metres. Eventually you will come to an outcrop of red sandstone with prehistoric cup and ring markings. The softness of the rock that enabled these carvings to be done by primitive tools also accounts for the depth of this gorge. Just after here you walk on rock between river and cliff. **In wet weather these rocks offer no grip at all to boots and it is like walking on ice. I strongly suggest that in wet weather you remove your boots and negotiate this**

20-metre stretch in your stockinged feet. Better wet feet than broken bones.

Shortly after this the valley widens and flattens. The path runs directly onto a cart track, which you follow straight ahead. Pass a gate by the stile on its left. Go right over a footbridge and then left and right through a farmyard. Turn right onto a minor tarmac road after the farmyard and proceed for 20 metres. Go left onto a minor road where a sign points to a public footpath. Go right and uphill on a footpath immediately before the works. Cross the rudimentary stile and follow the edge of the wood left. Follow the wood's edge right uphill at the end of the field. Cross another stile at the top left-hand corner of the field. Turn left along the hedge and go over another stile onto a footpath between a wood and a fence. Bear around to the right with this then walk right up the tarmac road where the path terminates. Walk to your right up this.

About 300 metres up this road, as you approach the graveyard on your right, bypass a minor road on the right and go left onto another minor road just after this. Follow this road through several minor curves and then sharply right, left and right to a T-junction. The Burns monument comes into sight ahead and to the right.

If you are visiting the monument: at the junction, proceed right along the B743 for nearly 200 metres. Take the second road on the left, just before the railway embankment. This is signposted 'Bogwood'. About 200 metres up here go right on the cart track under the railway then bear left immediately after the bridge, as guided by the public footpath sign. At the end of this track, climb over the gate (it was tied with barbed wire) and go along the right-hand edge of the field. Go over a stile and then along the right-hand edge of the next field. At the top of the hill climb the first gate and go over the stile to the right of the second gate. Go right along the tarmac farm drive to the Burns monument. Return to the junction after your visit.

If you are not visiting the monument, cross the minor road and walk the 20 metres down the lane to the main road, the A76(T). Turn left along the main road and, after about 100 metres – having past the garage and garden centre – go right along a minor road. About 100 metres along here veer right with the road and pass Hillhead Farm on the left. Approximately 100 metres after the farm the road bends sharply right, then goes left about 150 metres after this. At this point there is a stile to the left of a farm gate on your right. Having crossed the stile and gone directly ahead you will find another stile, again on the left of a field gate.

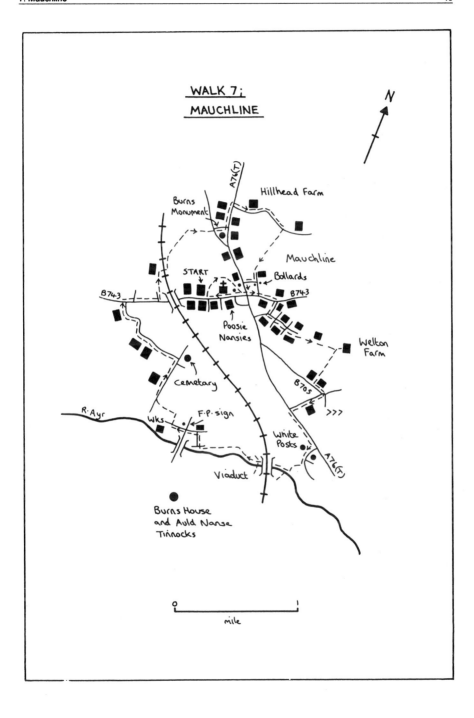

WALK 7;
MAUCHLINE

N

A76(T)

Hillhead Farm

Burns
Monument

Mauchline

START

Bollards

B743

B743

Poosie
Nansies

Welton
Farm

B705

Cemetary

R·Ayr

F·P·sign

>>>

Wks

White
Posts

A76(T)

Viaduct

Burns House
and Auld Nanse
Tinnocks

0   1
mile

Keeping the hedge to your left, descend this field to another stile in the extreme left-hand corner.

Proceed ahead between garage and fence. Follow this path around to the left and go straight ahead as it becomes a concrete walkway. Take the last concrete walkway on the right before the path comes to a dead end. At the T-junction, turn left along the tarmac road and walk to the bollards. Here go right down a lane to the main road. Walk left along the main road, past the fire station and to the lights. Here go right. On your left, about 50 metres past the lights, is Poosie Nansie's Tavern. In the winter of 1785/6 Burns wrote about the Jolly Beggars after witnessing them here. Poosie Nansie was Agnes Gibson, the landlady here. Opposite this on your right is the entrance to Mauchline Churchyard, where numerous contemporaries of Burns are buried including Gavin Hamilton, Holy Willie, the Gaud Boy and Poosie Nansie. The graves are marked with little metal plaques. Beyond here on the right is the Loudon Arms.

Poosie Nansie's Tavern

8. Failford

Route: Failford – Highland Mary's Monument – Forest Walk – Coilsfield Mains – Bachelors' Club – Coilsfield

Distance: 5 miles

Map: OS Landranger 70, Ayr, Kilmarnock

Start: Failford Inn

Access: By bus: there is no direct service from Glasgow. Take the express bus to Ayr bus station – it is a reasonable service. From Ayr bus station take a local bus, a moderately frequent service, to Tarbolton. Ring 0141 332 7133 or 0141 333 1100 for details. By car: take the M8 westbound and towards the airport out of Glasgow centre. Come off at junction 22 to join the M77 for Kilmarnock. When this ends, continue on the A77 (T). At Bogend, shortly after bypassing Kilmarnock, turn left onto the B730, signposted to Tarbolton. When you reach the A719 go right along this for about half a mile then pick up the B730 on your left, heading for Tarbolton. About a mile down here go sharply left and then right, into and straight through Tarbolton. About a mile after Tarbolton you come to a four-way junction with the B 743 to Failford. Go left here. After about a mile and a half you pass under a railway bridge. The Failford Inn is about 250 metres beyond this on your right. There is a smallish car park on the left-hand side of the road.

The Bachelors' Club

This is a 17th-century thatched house. When Burns and his family moved to Tarbolton (pronounced Tarbowton) in 1777 this was John Richard's alehouse. Lots of village social functions were held in the first-floor room.

In 1780 Robert Burns, his brother Gilbert and five other young men held the first meeting of their Bachelors' Club here. This was a debating club to relieve the monotony of their daily lives. The most that they were allowed to spend was 3d, which would have bought six pints in those days. So it was not a club for dissipation. All members had to be professed lovers of one or more of the female sex. If a member married he could stay in the club if the majority agreed. The club met every

The Bachelors Club

fourth Monday night. Obscene and profane language was banned. The character of the members was to be open-hearted and helpful, not avaricious or petty-spirited.

Their first debate concerned whether a man without money, if given a choice of women, should marry the one with money or the one without. In 1784 Burns left Tarbolton for Mauchline where he started an almost identical club. Without the driving force of Burns behind it the Bachelors' Club of Tarbolton declined and died.

The building was altered for housing in the early 19th century. Just before the Second World War it was in a tumbledown state and was to have been pulled down. However, the National Trust bought and renovated it. It is now filled with furniture and artefacts of the Burns era. On the 25th of January each year a Burns Supper is held here. Entrance to the Bachelors' Club is free if you are a member of the National Trust, otherwise there is a small charge. It is worth a visit as the guide is knowledgeable and entertaining. It is open most afternoons. For more details of opening hours phone 01292 541940.

The Walk

Turn left out of the Failford Inn and cross the bridge on the road. Just over the bridge a sign on your right points left to the Failford Gorge. Go down here on the path. If you turn right and go behind the Failford Gorge sign a grassy path leads to a kissing gate. A flagged path then leads you to the monument commemorating Robert Burns meeting with Highland Mary. A plaque at the monument tells the story.

Having turned left into Failford Gorge, walk down this path for 50 metres until it forks – here go left. Between this path and the river is a great deal of giant hogweed. These are six-foot tall plants with parasols of white flowers on top and maroon stems. Do not touch this – **it is poisonous**. Continue along this path and cross a footbridge. About 100 metres beyond the footbridge the path forks. Go right at this point and follow the steps uphill and along the valley side with the River Ayr below and left of you. You arrive at a notice giving you details of the Ayr Gorge Woodlands Wildlife Reserve. Retrace your steps about 20 metres to go diagonally left onto a new path there. This becomes a cart track. As you approach the cottage on your left, veer right with the track until it comes to the main road. In summer these woods are filled with herb Robert – the small, five-petalled, pink geranium.

At the road turn left under the lovely old red sandstone railway bridge. This is a listed building. The red sandstone used to be quarried locally in Mauchline. About 50 metres beyond the bridge turn right onto a farm track immediately before the woods on the right. Follow this enclosed track for about half a mile until you reach a four-way junction. Turn right here, keeping the woods on your left. Cross a footbridge and go through a gate, closing it behind you please. Continue with this track, heading across fields towards a wood on the skyline. Go through a kissing gate on the left of a farm gate and skirt a wood on your left.

When the track makes a T-junction with a minor road, go left along the road towards Tarbolton, which is on a hill ahead and to the left of you. There is an oddity on the right on this road: a beech tree with the silver bark of a birch. Walk along the road for about a quarter of a mile then go to the right at the four-way junction and into Tarbolton. Bear left around the Black Bull and go down Montgomery Street. Down here on your left is a Masonic Hall. If the caretaker is there you may be able to see the actual regalia and accoutrements that Robert Burns used when he was received into the order here.

At the foot of Montgomery Street, where the road bends sharply left,

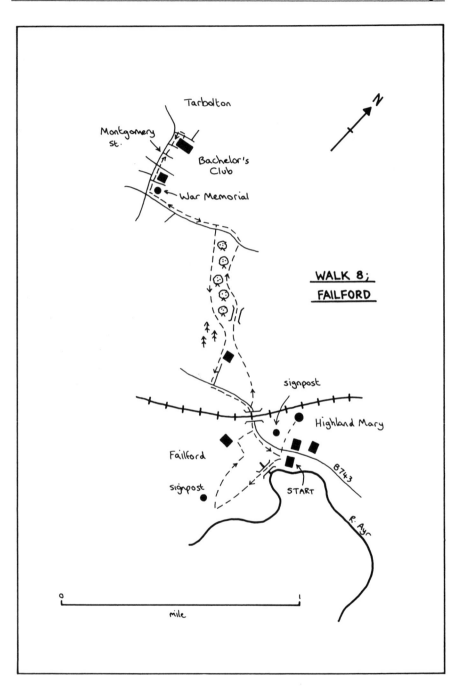

Tarbolton

Montgomery St.

Bachelor's Club

War Memorial

WALK 8;
FAILFORD

signpost

Highland Mary

Failford

B743

signpost

START

R. Ayr

0   1

mile

a brown National Trust for Scotland sign points you right to the Bachelors' Club. Walk back down Montgomery Street, past the Black Bull and the bus stop to the War memorial. Here turn left down the minor road. About a quarter of a mile down here take the unmade road on the right which you can see going along the right-hand edge of the woods. Follow this, it eventually becomes a footpath along the edge of the wood. Shortly after it becomes a track again it bends tightly right. At this point go left onto a tarmac path through grass. A concrete fence post spans a ditch here, functioning as a primitive footbridge. Cross this to a semi-tarmac path on its other side. Keep on this as it leads between conifers on the right and deciduous trees on the left, and then between woods and a fence.

At the end of the woods is a four-way junction. Turn right uphill on the farm road here. At the farm go straight ahead on the tarmac, bypassing the farm on your left. Stay with this road as it bends left and right. At the T-junction with the B743 turn left along it. Approximately 200 metres later turn right immediately after going under the railway bridge. About 10 metres up the drive to Coilswood Cottage go left onto a footpath. Follow this, in places overgrown, path for about 300 metres as it runs parallel with the road. At the end of the woods, where the River Ayr is in sight ahead, the path forms a T-junction with another. Go left here and up to the road. Turn right onto the road and cross the bridge. The Failford Inn is on your right.

9. The High Road, Luss

Route: Luss—Auchengavin—Edentaggart—Glenmollochan—Tom na Glas

Distance: 4½ miles

Map: OS Landranger 56, Loch Lomond and Inveraray

Start: The Colquhoun Arms, Luss

Access: Luss is 20 miles north-west of Glasgow city centre, on the west side of Loch Lomond. By bus: this is possible if you pick your arrival and departure times carefully. Luss is on the Glasgow to Fort William bus route and two companies run services: Scottish Citylink 0990 505050 and Martins Coaches 01397 712579/772042. By train: ring Rail Enquiries on 0345 484950 for details. Trains do not run to Luss but it is possible to get a train with a connecting local bus service. If you are considering taking a ferry across the loch to Luss be warned that they are not running in 1998. Check carefully! By car: this is the easiest option as there are now good roads all the way. Take the A82 westbound out of Glasgow. It is signposted to Loch Lomond and/or Crianlarich. After about 20 miles of dual carriageway and other good roads you will see a signpost pointing right towards Luss. Drive down this (the old Loch Lomondside road) for nearly two miles. As you arrive in Luss the Colquhoun Arms is on your left. It has a goodly amount of space in its car park. In the unlikely event of you not finding space here, there is a large free car park signposted to your right about 100 metres further on.

The Colquhoun Arms

This pub is over 200 years old and was originally a coaching inn. The horse troughs are still in the cellars at the back of the building. Queen Victoria's coach changed horses here as she drove from Inveraray to Balloch. Samuel Taylor Coleridge and William and Dorothy Wordsworth also stayed here overnight on the 24th of August 1803. It is now a listed building.

The name Colquhoun Arms comes from the fact that this was historically land owned by the Colquhoun clan. The sign outside is bilingual, having the inn's name in both English and Gaelic. Inside it is a very pleasant bar. There is an attractive mixture of light wood, brickwork, wallpaper and carpets. Decor includes brass, dried flowers, pictures of local scenes, maps and old inn notices. There is a real fire in winter. Lots of walkers use this pub, particularly at weekends, so it used to coping with and catering for ramblers.

Miss Maitz, the landlady, assures me that it offers the best value-for-money food on the loch side, and I have no reason to disagree with her. Take a good appetite as the portions are huge. Their haggis is very popular. Food is served from 12.00 to 21.00 seven days a week. Bar opening hours are 11.00 to 23.00 Monday to Saturday, and 12.30 to 23.00 on Sundays. There are only keg beers available. McEwans 70/- and 80/-, McEwans Lager, Miller, John Smiths, Guinness, Murphys and Strongbow are the pumps on offer. Telephone 01436 860 282.

The Colquhoun Arms

Luss

This is an outstandingly picturesque village in an incredibly scenic setting on the shore of Loch Lomond. The history of Luss is largely that of the Colquhoun clan. Luss has been here since the 13th century. The Colquhouns originally acquired these lands as a reward for loyalty to Robert the Bruce. The fourth Laird of Colquhoun reinforced his hold on this area by marrying the Fair Maid of Luss. She was the heiress to this estate and a member of the old Celtic nobility that had previously held this fief. Robert the Bruce also granted Luss the right of gyrth (sanctuary for wanted criminals), in honour of St Kessog who worked here. The Colquhouns' castle was at Rossdhu (a Gaelic name meaning 'black-wooded promontory'), a couple of miles south of Luss.

In 1603 the MacGregors from across the loch pillaged and plundered Luss, and subsequently slaughtered the Colquhouns in Glen Fruin (Glen of Sorrow) at the south edge of the loch. The MacGregor chiefs were then judicially murdered and the clan proscribed, having their lands taken away from them. It was a criminal offence to call yourself MacGregor, and helping or sheltering any of this hapless clan was subject to severe penalties. The MacGregors have ever since been known as 'The Children of the Mist and Snow'. The looting and murder was fairly normal behaviour at this time but the MacGregors' real crime was being directly descended from Malcolm Canmore (Bighead), first king of a united Scotland. Their clan motto is 'Royal is my Race'. In fact, at many times, in genealogical terms, the MacGregor Chief had a better claim to the throne of Scotland than the incumbent.

When the tourists first arrived in Luss, residents would camp out in tents in the summer while letting out their dwellings.

'High Road'

Because Luss is such a beautiful village and close to Glasgow it was chosen to be the setting of the TV soap opera 'High Road'. Luss is Glendarroch and Ben Lomond is Ben Darroch. While most of the series is shot indoors in studios in Glasgow, if you go in winter or early summer you may see STV shooting outside scenes here. If you watch this series you will recognise the church and the shop and post office near the pier. Both locations are used in this series and are on this walk. Apparently, sometimes you can come across members of the cast showing fans around 'their village'.

Because of extraneous noises, weather or tourists in the background it can take as much as an hour to get a take lasting a minute into the can. Once they were almost finished, watched by 300 Japanese tourists, when 300 flashbulbs went off as one and they had to start again from the beginning. If they are at work when you are there please co-operate with the crew.

The Walk

Leave the Colquhoun Arms and turn left along the old Loch Lomondside road through the village. After about 100 metres turn right into the clearly signed car park. In the car park there is a visitor centre where you can collect information about the area.

Exit the car park on the opposite side from the Visitor Centre, keeping to the left of the Farm Milk Bar. Go down Murray Place to the T-junction at its far end. There turn left down Glenburn Court. Go left at the four-way junction down here, keeping Highland Arts and the post office on your right. This should look familiar to fans of 'High Road'. Head down towards the pier. The cottages were built in a style dictated by a dowager Lady Colquhoun. Villages like this do not just happen; they are created. This helps explain why Luss is a conservation village. At the pier walk to your right along the rough road with the loch on your left. Then turn right again up another rough road just before the churchyard wall.

Proceed through the lych-gate on your left and into the graveyard. Walk to your half right with the church on your left. There is an 11th-century Norse hog's back gravestone straight ahead of you.

St Kessog, an Irish monk, is supposedly buried here. In the era of Burke and Hare two parishioners spent every night here in a tent to protect bodies against resurrectionists. This church appears in 'High Road'.

Leave the churchyard by the gate you arrived through and go straight ahead on the minor road. Walk along past the coffee shop on your left. At the T-junction at the end turn left and walk up to the Colquhoun Arms. Go left along the road in front of the hotel. Walk past the Luss Highland Gathering field on your left. Just after this, double back right on the poorly surfaced track at Woodlands Cottage, which is also on the right. At the end of this track go through the kissing gate and up the steps to the main road. Head right for about 20 metres and then go left at the sign for 'Darroch'. Immediately take the right-hand fork, signposted for Hill of Camstradden Farm.

Walk through the farmyard and keep going on the farm track, easing gently uphill. Wander around the isolated house and go through two sets of gates in line ahead and to the left of the barn. Follow the track along the contour of the hill. Cross a stream by stepping stones then go half left uphill to a field gate. Once through this continue along the cart track and across a very small stream.

The cart track now dies out. Look for a ditch with a small earth dyke on its valley side contouring along the hillside ahead. It is obviously not natural as it's in a straight line. You follow this along the hillside. Often your path is along the top of this two-foot high dyke. After about one and a half miles you arrive at a fence across your path. The fence ahead of you at the end of the dyke is the one bit of this fence without a top strand of barbed wire.

Cross this and carefully negotiate the steep-sided little valley beyond it. Once on the other side, climb over a piece of fencing ahead of you that looks like a field gate but is not hung or hinged. Follow the fence on your right along the contour line. After about half a mile you come to a field gate in the fence – this is about 50 metres before the fence peters out after a second field gate.

Go through the first field gate and right downhill to find the footbridge over the river. Follow the track on the other side of the footbridge through rough pasture to find a gate. This gate leads onto a rough road that is fenced on both sides. Proceed right down here. Please close the gate behind you.

Keep on the road over a bridge. At this point it becomes a metalled road. Walk past the entrance to Glenmollochan Farm and continue on this road. This is an extremely quiet road serving only half a dozen farms and coming to a dead end. It is more like a tarmac footpath and it is entirely possible that you will see no traffic at all on it.

Glenmollochan Farm was, in 1749, the first place in the Highlands to farm black-faced sheep. This led to the Highland Clearances and the demise of the rearing of black cattle in the Highlands. After this beef became an expensive luxury instead of the everyday food it had been before. And Scots learned how to make Scotch broth and mutton pies!

Walk down this road for the next two miles. As you go, notice the forest to your right. The old Caledonian Forest must have been something like this before it was destroyed. Just after the cattle grid at the main Loch Lomondside road turn left up the minor tarmac road. Keep on this to find the pedestrian overpass. Take either path once across the road as they both end up at the same place. When the path hits a tarmac road, turn right. In the field on your right there are often little Shetland ponies. When you reach the main road through Luss turn right. The Colquhoun Arms is 100 metres up on your right-hand side.

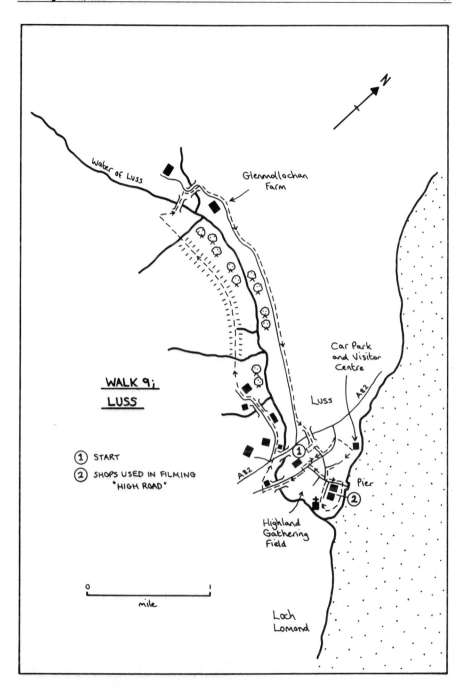

WALK 9;
LUSS

① START
② SHOPS USED IN FILMING
"HIGH ROAD"

Water of Luss

Glenmollochan
Farm

Car Park
and Visitor
Centre

A82

Luss

A82

Pier

Highland
Gathering
Field

Loch
Lomond

0
mile

10. Milngavie

Route: Milngavie – Craigallian Loch – Easter Carbeth – Arlehaven – Ardoch – Craigend Castle – Mugdock Castle – Mugdock Wood

Distance: 8 miles

Map: OS Landranger 64, Glasgow

Start: The Cross Keys, Milngavie

Access: The easiest way to get to this walk is by rail. The official start of the West Highland Way (WHW) is Milngavie station and it is signposted from the station. The Cross Keys is on the brief walk (via a pedestrian underpass and precinct) from the station to the WHW proper. There are regular train services to Milngavie (pronounced Mullguy) from Glasgow Queen Street, low level – even on a Sunday. Timetable enquiries 0345 484950. There are also plenty of buses. By car: from Glasgow take the A81 for Aberfoyle. On the outskirts of Milngavie take the B8030 at the roundabout. Shortly after this becomes a dual carriageway you arrive at a set of traffic lights – the entrance to Tesco's car park is on your right. Turn left here up Ellangowan Road, signposted for Mugdock. Go under the footbridge and past the bus stop on your left. Turn right where the sign says car park and right again into the car park. Parking is free. Exit the car park with Ellangowan Road at your back and turn right past the public toilets on your left. The Cross Keys is 30 metres down on your left. The Cross Keys is hoping to get the pub signposted from the main road soon. By the time that you read this it may be possible to follow Cross Key signposts from the centre of Milngavie to the pub.

The Cross Keys

There has been a pub on this site for about 200 years, but not always called the Cross Keys. The owners of the Cross Keys have a pub at each end of the WHW: the Cross Keys in Milngavie at the start and the Ben Nevis in Fort William at its end. Some pub-crawl that would be. For those who manage this pub-crawl the owners are thinking of offering something commemorative, such as a T-shirt proclaiming 'I've done the WHW'.

In the 1950s one of the staff from a local zoo used to ride Charlie the elephant down to this pub for a drink and leave him in the yard. It caused chaos and consternation when Charlie got bored one night and decided to go and see his friend in the pub. The story is that to this day there is a crack in the back wall of the pub.

It has just had £500,000 worth of refurbishment The interior is delightful, with beams, dark wood, light-coloured plaster, old books, bottles, photographs and a map of the WHW painted on a wall.

Scott Fraser, the manager, is pleased to see walkers. For early birds the pub is open from 10.00 for coffee and scones. This is definitely a pub to go to when you are hungry. There is a large selection of food: starters, main courses, grills (including steaks), vegetarian choices and salads as well as desserts. Food is served from 12.00 to 21.30 Monday to Saturday and from 12.30 until 21.30 on Sundays. If you go by train you can walk up an appetite to do justice to the food and stuff yourself with drink as well if you want.

Opening hours are 10.00 (coffee only at first) to 23.00 Monday to Thursday and 10.00 to 24.00 Friday and Saturday. Sundays it is 12.30 to 11.00. Deuchars IPA and Theakstons Best Bitter were the real ales on tap but the manager is planning to put on another pump of real ale, probably a varying guest beer. In keg were McEwans 70/-, Miller Pilsner, Guinness, Becks, John Smiths Extra Smooth, McEwans Lager and Strongbow. Telephone 0141 956 4211.

Mugdock Country Park

These 200 hectares (500 acres) are mainly woodland and include Mugdock Wood, a Site of Special Scientific Interest. Its interest lies in it being typical of the woodland that covered this countryside in ancient times. The trees are oak, birch and alder, with a scattering of rowan, elm and ash where the ground is less boggy. The oaks show signs of post coppicing such as multi-trunks. In coppicing the tree is cut down to provide a multiplicity of new shoots for fencing, for bark to produce tannic acid to convert raw hide into leather and to provide the basic material for the charcoal burner. Most of the trees have honeysuckle growing on them, which makes this a sweetly scented summer woodland haven. Mugdock Castle was the ancestral home of the Grahams, the lairds of Mugdock from the 13th century. They were known as the 'Gallant Grahams' and were staunch supporters of Robert the Bruce in the Wars of Independence. The original stone castle was built around 1372

The start of the West Highland Way, Milngavie

and was a square building with turrets at the corners and a central courtyard. In 1874 most of the building that remained was destroyed for it to be replaced with a country house. However, the south-west tower was saved and used as a smoking room.

The castle and its lands came into the possession of Sir Hugh Fraser, the department store magnate, after the Second World War. Afterwards they were given to the Central Regional Council, who laid out the country park in 1981.

Craigend Castle was built around 1820. The visitor centre at Mugdock Country Park is in the old stable block. The ancestral owners of this area were the Smith family. Originally tenants of the Grahams from around 1500, in 1670 they were allowed to buy this land because of their loyal service to the Grahams. Following the Second World War this land was sold to the Wilsons and they established the forerunner of Britain's safari parks. In completely open paddocks, grazing animals such as deer, bison, llamas and wild white cattle roamed freely. While cranes mingled with the patrons. A particular favourite was Charlie the elephant. At 5.5 tons he was the largest elephant in captivity and was very attached to his mahout (handler). They died on the same day. When the zoo closed in 1956 Charlie was set to become about 20,000 tins of pet food until Billy Butlin provided him with a home for life at Filey.

The Walk

Come out of the Cross Keys, turn left away from the car park and then go immediately right. Ahead of you is the pyramid that marks the start of the WHW. Go over the bridge and turn right at the pyramid. Follow the waymarkers (thistle) up the river. The WHW is only spasmodically waymarked, so apart from this opening few hundred yards you cannot rely on waymarking alone.

When you reach the footbridge over the river on your left go straight ahead, keeping the river on your near left. Approximately 200 metres beyond this a waymarker guides you right and uphill. Just over the top of the ridge a waymarker and a right of way sign to Mugdock Wood take you left on a wide, well-made path.

Follow this path along the hillside, keeping the river on your left and ignoring paths to left and right. Cross a burn and enter Mugdock Country Park. Keep with this dirt road for about a mile until you reach a metalled road where a WHW signpost guides you left. After about 20 metres go right through a chain stile; a sign here tells you that it is WHW.

After about half a mile you come to Craigallian Loch on your right, a blue jewel set in a fold of the hills. Continue up the left-hand side of the loch on the path straight ahead of you. Just past the end of the wood and the chalets on your left a waymarker guides you right. Buzzards are commonly seen here. The Khyber Pass Road you see signposted here is so-called because it had to be blasted out of solid rock. At the end of the path you will meet a tarmac road. Here a WHW signpost directs you left along the road. After about 200 metres a signpost on your right takes you up a grassy track between drystone dykes. Go over the stone stile in the dyke at the end of the track and proceed along the well-surfaced and very obvious path ahead.

Just after the isolated house of Arlehaven, a waymarker points left for the WHW. Ignore this and go straight ahead. This is where this walk leaves the WHW. Listen for the whistling diminuendo of the curlew here, sometimes they fly over this path. From here there are stunning views to the Campsies ahead and the Highlands on your left. After about 300 metres you come to a gate at the end of a conifer plantation on your left. Go through the gate and turn right, following the road around.

When you come to a tarmac road turn right and immediately right again. Go over the stile by the chevrons. Follow the fence and telegraph poles on your right uphill to reach some climbable fence at the next road. I could not find a stile at the other end of this path. If you want, you can just go right up the road and dog-leg round right with it to reach the top end of this field. The path you want will be on your left at the top of the hill.

Once over the fence there is a footpath signposted for Mugdock Country Park almost straight across the road. This path was signposted by the Scottish Rights of Way Society. At the top of the hill follow the path left and then right where it indicates a public footpath. This foot-path ends at a cart track. Go over the stile and right along the track, fol-lowing the sign for Mugdock Country Park. Go over a step stile by a gate and keep on this road. At the junction keep straight ahead, following signs for Mugdock Country Park. After about a mile, at a gate across the road, turn left as the public footpath sign directs. At the tarmac road go over the step stile and turn left up the road. Go round to the right on this road until you reach the visitor centre on your right – go in here.

The visitor centre is reached by descending into the enclosed court-yard. This has displays, information about the park, gift and craft shops and a tearoom. The visitor centre is open 09.00 to 17.00 every day. The tea shop is open from 11.00 to 17.00, with longer hours in summer. For more information phone 0141 956 6100.

Leave the visitor centre by the stone archway and go straight ahead along the dirt/gravel road. Follow the track past Craigend Castle. There was a Milngavie doctor who advised his patients that instead of taking sea air they should amble up to Craigend and breathe the clean air of the Highlands from the castle walls. About 600 metres past Craigend take the path on the right signposted to Mugdock Castle and Loch. Go across the sleeper bridge traversing the bog. Turn right at the T-junction where the arrow points you to Mugdock Castle. The most famous resident of this castle was the Earl of Montrose, the Great Marquis, a seminal figure in the Scottish religious reformation wars.

At the end of the road past the castle, turn right, leaving the castle be-hind you. Next turn immediately left, and then after 20 metres turn right again. These last two turns are signposted for Mugdock Wood and Drumclog Moor. Go through the narrow gate into Mugdock Wood and tread the interestingly surfaced path – in quick succession it is gravel, stone, gravel, stone, sleepers and beaten earth. When you come to a signpost directing you straight ahead to Drumclog Moor, take the path on the left. At the bottom of the hill turn left onto the WHW. At the fork by the blue seat follow the path to the right. At the T-junction turn left, keeping the Allander Water on your right. This rejoins the WHW and you follow this back to Milngavie and the Cross Keys.

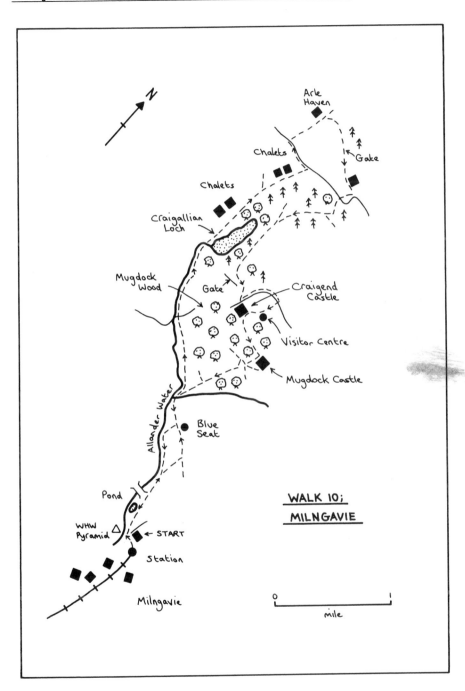

WALK 10;
MILNGAVIE

11. Dumgoyne

Route: Dumgoyne – Laigh Parks -High Lettre -Cantywheery – Blanefield – Arlehaven – Dumgoyach Farm

Distance: 8 miles

Map: OS Landranger 64, Glasgow

Start: Beech Tree Inn, Dumgoyne

Access: Dumgoyne is about 13 miles more or less due north of Glasgow. By car: take the A81, signposted for Aberfoyle, north out of Glasgow. The villages of Strathblane and Blanefield are contiguous. Go through these and follow this road along past the unmissably signposted Glengoyne Distillery three miles further on, on your right. Go past the road on the right that forks off to Killearn. About 200 metres after this the Beech Tree is on your left. There is ample car parking. There is an infrequent bus service from Glasgow. Ask to be put off at the Beech Tree. Alternatively, get the bus to Stirling via Balfron and get off at the Glengoyne Distillery then walk the 300 metres to the Beech Tree. It is the white building ahead and to the left of you. Timetable enquiries 01324 613777.

The Beech Tree Inn

This building is about 130 years old. It was on the railway line that is now part of the West Highland Way. For much of that time it was a grocer's shop. In 1976 Jimmy Gibb and his father took it over and converted it into the superb inn that it is now. This pub was a finalist in the Pub of the Year Awards run by the Scottish Licensed Trade Association in 1996 and 1997.

There was a huge beech tree outside from which the inn took its name, but a couple of years after the Gibbs took over it got sick and bits started falling off. To make things safe it was felled, in an operation that closed the main road outside for a while. The tree, sadly, was only 170 years old.

This is the place for celebrity spotters; it seems to attract weel kent faces. In 1963, when it was still a grocer's, Mrs Nielsen served four young lads from Liverpool with cheese. They were the Beatles. Liz Taylor has had a drink here. Larry Hagman and his wife had a meal here after visiting the Glengoyne Distillery. And Robbie Coltrane calls in now and then for a drink or a meal as he lives locally.

Jimmy Gibb is happy to see walkers in his bar. The long, narrow bar has pictures of the area in olden times on its walls. These include the old grocer's shop and Rob Roy's Tree, which used to stand beside the road down past the Glengoyne Distillery. It is said that Rob Roy eluded the Duke of Montrose by hiding in it. There are also colonial-style chairs, pictures of wildlife and flowers, lots of wildlife china plates, maps of the West Highland Way and lovely tapestry pictures of flowers. There is a butterfly lounge with cases of preserved butterflies and butterfly pictures. There is also a beer garden and children's playground.

The real ale is St Andrew's. Keg beers are Belhaven Best, Tennents Special, Tennents Lager, Guinness and also Dry Blackthorn Cider. Opening hours are 11.00 to 23.00 Monday to Saturday and 12.30 to 23.00 on Sundays. The food is traditional Scottish, including salmon from Loch Lomond. It is all home-cooked, fresh produce. It is served all day to 21.00 in summer. In winter it is served 12.00 to 14.30 and 17.00 to 21.00 seven days a week. Telephone 01360 550 297.

Strathblane

In Roman times Strathblane (the valley not the village) was occupied by the Damnonii. These Cymric people of the Celtic race originally came from Central Europe. Their land was called Y-Gogledd, the North. Later it was known as Cumbria or Strathclyde. Strathblane lies in a part of this area called Reged or Mureiff. This latter word shows connections with the roman word 'murus' meaning 'wall'. The Antonine Wall was not far south of here.

Legend has it that this was the home of King Arthur. After the Romans left this was a civilised and settled land, which he defended from Saxon barbarians. Merlin was a poet of Tweeddale. Other poets who sang of King Arthur were Llywrch Hen and Taliesen, both poets of Eastern Strathblane. Arthur was Guledig or war leader of Strathclyde and his famed twelve battles were fought in western Scotland. Kay, Galahad, Lancelot etc. were Celtic warriors of this region. Later these tribes migrated to Wales and Cornwall and took their legends with them in the form of oral poetry. Evidence to support this occurs in local place names such as Ben Arthur, The Cobbler.

This area, then known as Lennox, was incorporated into Scotland in 1034. The name Lennox comes from Levenach, which in turn comes from the River Leven. This area became part of the Earldom of Lennox. The Earl of Lennox, of the old Celtic nobility, was one of Robert the Bruce's supporters. Bruce was of mainly Norman descent.

Strathblane village's main industry was a calico printing works established in 1793. The work mainly involved blue dyeing. In 1823 twelve block printers were bought, employing 50 people. This was soon increased to 60 block printers employing 200/250 people. New dyes and machinery increased the workforce to its peak of 500 people in 1856. However, the centre of the cotton industry moved to Lancashire and carriage prices soon hit profits. Pollution problems did not help either. The works were closed at the end of the 19th century.

Glengoyne Distillery

This name means 'glen of the wild geese'. The stillman's art was first brought to Scotland by monks. By 1644 whisky production was wide-

Glengoyne Distillery

spread and the Scottish Parliament imposed duty on it. Whisky has been made here legally since 1833, although at one time there were 18 illicit stills in this one small valley alone. The exciseman used to live in a cottage here to ensure that all taxes were paid. In fact, Marshal of the Royal Air Force, Lord Tedder was born here while his father was the customs officer. And it was a taxman at Glengoyne who first devised the standards that have made Scotch world-renowned.

Glengoyne is a unique malt whisky in that it is unpeated. The malting process, unlike that of other whiskies, is not stopped by drying the malt over peat fires. As the water in the Glengoyne Burn flows directly there over volcanic rock, the water is also peat free. Telephone 01360 550 254.

The Walk

Come out of the Beech Tree, go into the car park then turn left to reach the main road. Go left along then cross the main road to go right on the disused railway line (thistle waymarker) about 20 metres past the Beech Tree. After about 400 metres this crosses a minor road. Turn right up the road. You are now leaving the West Highland Way. At the top of the hill turn right onto the main road. After about 100 metres past the speed limit and Killearn signs, turn left up a minor road marked Lettre. Lettre is famous for the quality of its black-faced sheep. Turn left just before the gate into the farmyard and go through another gate. Follow a track uphill for about 50 metres then go right along the cart track at the barn.

Follow this along the hillside for 3½ miles, enjoying views of the southern Highlands and the Blane Valley. The concrete structures you see along here are part of the aqueduct bringing water from Loch Katrine to Glasgow. Eventually this track becomes a metalled road and leads you into Strathblane. Turn right at the main road by the Blane Valley Inn. Go down the main road for 200 metres and then turn left where the signpost points to Stockiemuir, B821. At the top of the little hill, where the road dog-legs sharply left, go straight ahead on the cart track. Continue on this for about a quarter of a mile. When you arrive at the T-junction by the fir plantation go left, keeping the trees on your right. After about 300 metres, as the house comes into view, go right on a well-laid path where a thistle waymarker welcomes you to the West Highland Way. Just before the wooded hill of Dumgoyach on your right

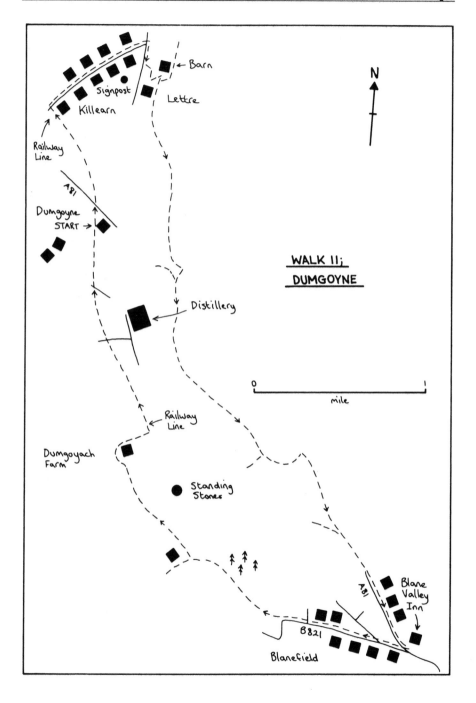

Barn

Signpost

Lettre

Killearn

Railway
Line

A81

Dumgoyne
START →

WALK 11;
DUMGOYNE

Distillery

0   1

mile

Railway
Line

Dumgoyach
Farm

Standing
Stones

Blane
Valley
Inn

A81

B821

Blanefield

N

are standing stones, also on your right. Here you may well see buzzards circling and mewing in the sky above you; they are quite common on this section of the West Highland Way. At Dumgoyach Farm a thistle waymarker guides down a track to the left of the farm. Just across the river turn left onto the disused railway track by a chain stile, following the thistle waymarker. After about half a mile you cross a minor road.

The large white building on the main road to your right front is the Glengoyne Distillery. A 200-metre detour along the minor then main road will take you there. It is possible to take a tour around the distillery for a small fee – starting with a tasting of the product. If you intend to do this I suggest that you take a polythene bag with you to put your muddy boots in while you do the tour.

Stay on the railway track after the minor road. A small ridge on your left can give less muddy walking. This marks the course of an aqueduct bringing water from Loch Lomond and the red and yellow brick structures along this are access points. About 300 metres along this you come across a sign giving you glad tidings of great joy: the Beech Tree Inn is approaching.

12. Drymen

Route: Drymen – Garadhban Forest – Milton of Buchanan – Buchanan Old House – Buchanan Home Farm

Distance: 7 miles

Map: OS Landranger 57, Stirling and the Trossachs

Start: Winnock Hotel, Drymen

Access: Drymen is about 15 miles north-north-west of Glasgow. The best way there by far is by car. Drive up the A809 from Glasgow through Milngavie. After about ten miles you pass the A811 to Dumbarton on the left and then cross the Endrick Water. (The bridge over the Endrick Water is worth a look. A Major Caulfield built this five-arched structure in 1765 to a General Wade design. It has subsequently been strengthened for traffic.) Once past these landmarks you will shortly see the B858 on your left, signposted for Drymen. As you drive into Drymen look for the signpost to Balmaha on your left. Turn left here and follow the road round right to reach the signposted car park of the Winnock Hotel on your right. There is an infrequent bus service to Drymen from Glasgow. Buses stop at the village green outside the Winnock Hotel. For details of services phone Midland Bluebird Busline 01324 613 777 or get a timetable from the travel centre in St Enoch's Square, Glasgow. (The travel centre building was designed by James Miller.)

The Winnock Hotel

This was a coaching inn but it is not nearly as old as the date carved in stone (1702) outside it suggests. This was done by a local carpenter with his tongue firmly in his cheek. The name Winnock means 'small windows'.

There is a flint floor in the bar and low beams so don't mind your muddy boots, watch your head instead. It is a lovely bar with metal scrollwork, metal range and fireplace and portraits of game birds on the wall. There is also a memorial to David Smith, shoemaker to gentlemen, from his friends. Behind the bar there are many rare old malt whiskies in a display case. Over 70 malt whiskies are available at this bar. There is a beer garden at the back. Dogs are restricted to the beer garden but children are allowed in the hotel, so John Carpendale the general manager tells me. The bar is open Monday to Thursday 11.00 to 24.00, Friday and Saturday 11.00 to 01.00 and on Sundays from 12.00 to 24.00. Real ales on draught are Tetley Bitter, Kanes Amber Ale and Merlins Ale. Keg on draught includes Calders 70/-, Calders Cream Ale, Tartan Special, Carlsberg Export, Tennents Lager, Guinness and Strongbow Dry Cider.

There is an excellent choice of good quality, well-priced food in the bar or restaurant. All produce is fresh and all meals are home cooked. Seafood is a speciality, especially from Loch Fyne. Finnan haddock and Loch Fyne salmon and kippers all feature on the menu. There is a cappuccino machine. Bar meals are served seven days a week from 12.00 to 21.30.

There is a petanque green out the back and bowls can be borrowed from reception. There is usually a member of staff around who knows how to play and can advise on the rules. On Tuesday nights (knights?) there is a medieval re-enactment on the village green outside. On this green on Thursday nights a pipe band plays.

The Winnock Hotel

Famous guests include Billy Connolly, who mentions Drymen in his latest video. Magnus Magnusson comes here for meetings of the Loch Lomond Forestry Commission. Marti Pellew from Wet, Wet, Wet also comes in a lot. Telephone 01360 660 245.

Drymen

In the past this was a cattle town, Scotland's Wild West. Rob Roy used to pass through here with rustled cattle, but most of Drymen's cattle business was legitimate. Highland cattle were driven south to market from here. In those days Highland cattle were black, not the brown colour that you see nowadays adorning chocolate boxes.

Cattle marts and fairs routinely took place in Drymen Square as long ago as the early 18th century. In 1767 up to eight fairs occurred here annually. The more juvenile segment of the population particularly enjoyed these. They featured tripping the light fantastic, sweetmeat stalls and target shooting. These slowly became less frequent until at the start of the 20th century only Drymen feeing fair remained, held biannually in May and November. Feeing fairs were where country employers and employees looked for workers and work respectively.

When the trains ran to Drymen much of their cargo was local milk. In those days, milkmaids were clad in striped aprons known as druggets. These were so called because they were made of rough woollen cloth named drugget. The cows were hand milked into wooden buckets known as luggies.

Drymen Church is also of note. This is listed as a building of special historic or architectural interest, category B. In 1986 a sealed box in a neighbourhood bank was unlocked as no one knew what was in it. In the box were found two silver vessels. One was engraved Communion Cup of the Kirk of Drymen 1732, and the other Kirk of Drymen 1852. In the 1880s these vessels had been donated to the church and put in the bank vaults for safety. Over the years they had slipped from everyone's memory!

The Walk

Exit the Winnock Hotel on the opposite side from its car park. Walk across the village green and up the B road to Stirling ahead of you. Go between the Gift Box on your left and the Spar on your right. Just past the police station on your left, also on your left, you will find a pleasant

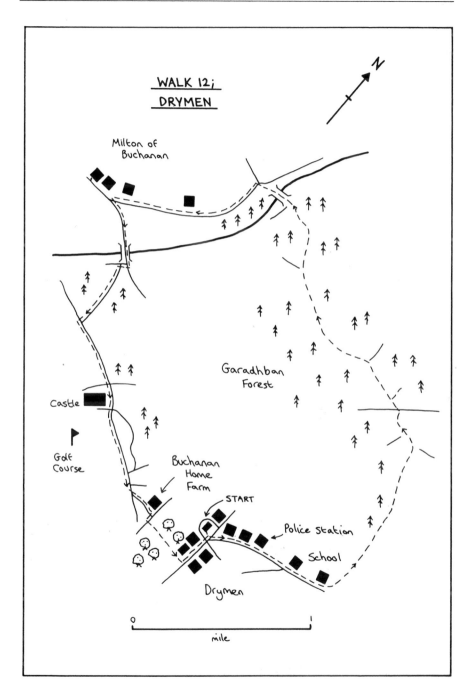

WALK 12;
DRYMEN

Milton of
Buchanan

Garadhban
Forest

Castle

Golf
Course

Buchanan
Home
Farm

START

Police Station

School

Drymen

0   1
mile

little path running parallel to the road but screened from it by bushes. Go up here over a bridge and past the school on your left. Here a West Highland Way (WHW) waymarker, a thistle, guides you onto a path between hedges running alongside the main A road to Stirling. After about 200 to 300 metres of this go briefly ahead along the main road. About 100 metres past Glenalva House a WHW signpost directs you left onto a footpath. This path runs beside a fence on your left and then goes through gorse bushes.

Go over a stile onto a fenced-in path. Go past a road to the right as guided by a WHW waymarker. At the T-junction at the top go left. Bypass a road to the left. In this section navigation is mainly a matter of following the WHW waymarkers. Turn left at the tarmac road and then right after about 20 metres. A sign informs you that you are now entering Gardhban Forest. Go directly ahead, ignoring a footpath on your right, then bypass another track on the right. Go right at the fork and then pass by another road on the left, still following the WHW waymarkers. Shortly after this, cross a decent-sized burn by a bridge before coming to a slightly offset four-way junction at the end of the forest.

Turn left downhill here, you have now left the WHW. Keep on this track all the way down to the tarmac road at the bottom of the hill in the hamlet Milton of Buchanan. This is about one mile. As you descend this hill you get good views over southern Loch Lomond and its islands. Turn left along the tarmac road. After about 200 metres cross a burn and turn right into a driveway. Five metres in turn left onto a rough road before the white gateposts. This is marked 'Private Road; No through Traffic'. This applies only to cars, not you – this is Scotland after all. Go past some houses. The Dobermann here is noisy but she just barked at me. Follow this road around to the right through a forest until you arrive at a T-junction. Turn left here then cross a bridge. If you come here in the right season you will see wild forget-me-nots growing on the bridge parapet. Go through and ahead at a 4-way junction with a sign 'Roadcare, Vehicles 15mph, Horses walking pace.'

At the next 4-way junction, where there is a small castle on your right, go diagonally left uphill. About 300 metres along here, after the last cottage and at the second 'Rohallion' sign on your right, go left down the minor tarmac road. Keep down here until a T-junction with another tarmac road. Go left along this. Along here take the second turning on the left, opposite Strathendrick view on the right. Go through a gate on this farm road and through Buchanan Home Farm. Turn right

where you see the Lomondside Stud sign on y
smoke here. Walk down for about ten metres. Ju
your left is a footpath, also on the left. Walk throug
path.

This is a finch walk. While doing this walk I saw g.
finch, bullfinch and goldfinches. Perhaps you might see ɩ
cies of finch and better my tally.

Go over a stile onto an enclosed path twixt fences and hɩ ͺes. This
takes you over a slight rise and down to the main road. This path is in total about half a mile long from Buchanan Home Farm to the road. Turn
left along the road. About 200 metres up here the Winnock Hotel is on
your left.

13. Balmaha

Route: Balmaha—Conic Hill—Milarrochy Bay—Arrochymore Point—Craigie Fort

Distance: 4 miles

Map: OS Landranger 56, Loch Lomond and Inveraray

Start: Oak Tree Inn, Balmaha

Access: This walk is not really possible by public transport as there are no direct buses from Glasgow. If there are a group of you perhaps you could get a bus to Drymen and taxi the five miles to Balmaha. The taxi office in Drymen is by the village green. By car: Balmaha is on the south-eastern edge of Loch Lomond, about 20 miles north-west of Glasgow. From Glasgow city centre take the A82 westwards to Annieland Cross. Here go right on the A739 (Switchback) towards Bearsden and Milngavie. A couple of miles along here the road splits with the A81 going right for Milngavie. Go straight ahead on the A809. Follow this for about 12 miles until a sign on the left takes you into Drymen. As you arrive in Drymen village look for a signpost on the left for Balmaha. If you reach the village green you have missed it. Go down this for about five miles until you reach Balmaha. Once in the village the Oak Tree Inn is on your left. It has no car park but directly across the road from it is a well-signposted, huge free car park.

Oak Tree Inn

The Oak Tree Inn is brand new, having opened in November 1987. Mr and Mrs Fraser, the owners, had a dream for many years of opening something like this in Balmaha. They felt that walkers were poorly served in the area. So when a huge 300-year-old oak tree in the area crashed to the ground, this was the spur that they needed. The Oak Tree was built and the bar area walls, ceiling, beams, furniture etc. were made out of the tree. Panelling rescued from a nearby country house dating back to 1864 was also incorporated into the fabric of the Oak Tree. The exterior of this inn has beautifully slated walls. These slates are from a local quarry that briefly reopened for this very purpose. There is also a 500-year-old oak tree just outside the inn.

The pub is situated on the banks of Loch Lomond on the West Highland Way (WHW). As it was built for walkers, muddy boots, wet clothes and rucksacks are no problem. Indeed, half the bar floor is flagged. If you are thinking about walking the WHW this pub has bunkhouse accommodation.

The manager, Danny Hayes, has lived in the area for 14 years and knows it well. He says that the idea is to make the Oak Tree a local resource by doing that little bit more. And to make it into an institution on the WHW by doing that bit extra. He says that even if you just want to use the loos you are welcome to. The interior has prints of old Balmaha on the walls that come from local people's parents' and grandparents' photographs.

The food is good, well priced and offers plenty of choice. It is served from 08.00 to 21.30 seven days a week. There is also a restaurant. The opening hours (for beer) are 11.00 to 24.00 Monday to Thursday, 11.00 to 01.00 Fridays and Saturdays and 12.30 to 24.00 on Sundays. The resident real ale is Maclays Broadsword and there are also guest real ales. Keg beers include Guinness, Tennents Lager, Thistle 70/- and 80/-, Wallace and Stella Artois. There is also Strongbow Dry Cider on draught. Telephone 01360 870357/870440.

Balmaha

As you gaze on the peaceful and tranquil village that is today's Balmaha it is perhaps hard to imagine that a thriving chemical industry was once based here. From the early 1800s pyroligneous acid was manufactured here. This was used in the preparation of Turkey red, the main dye used in cotton printing. Scows or barges transported timber, mainly oak, from all over Loch Lomondside to Balmaha. After the timber was processed, these same boats took the pyroligneous acid in wooden barrels to the Millburn Works in the Vale of Leven, where Turnbull and Co. had their main plant. The River Leven takes the water from Loch Lomond into the Clyde. Other products of the Balmaha factory were tar, creosote, methyl alcohol, acetone and acetic acid. The factory closed in 1920, after Turkey red came to be produced synthetically.

The Dukes of Montrose held salmon netting rights at Balmaha. Salmon were caught twice a week from May to August. The 5th Duke of Montrose's steam yacht, The Lady Violet, pleasure cruised from

Path and Loch Lomond, from Balmaha

Balmaha. In the 1920s paddle steamers plied Loch Lomond from Balmaha. These were a lifeline for loch side and island communities.

The Walk

Depart from the Oak Tree and cross the road into the car park. There is a Visitor Centre here with information about the area. Proceed to the far right-hand corner of the car park. Turn right onto the path at the back of the car park, following a thistle waymarker of the West Highland Way (WHW) to join it.

Follow this path around to the left and right for about 200 metres then turn left off the path as guided by a thistle waymarker. Go up three sets of steps and through a kissing gate at the end of the wood. Follow the obvious path straight ahead. Keep on this path as it bears left. Go up more steps. About 50 metres beyond the top of these go left as indicated by the waymarker. Turn right uphill at the next waymarker, which is on a small knoll. At the next waymarker, where you can see the WHW ahead crossing the left of Conic Hill, hairpin half back and left on the well-defined grassy path. Follow this path along the ridge top towards Loch Lomond. The path can fade in and out but if you keep to the northern (right-hand) side of this ridge you will soon pick up a very good path.

About halfway down this ridge, a prominent, parallel rocky spur comes into sight on your right. A path takes you the 20 metres across to the start of this. Now you just follow the well-worn path atop this spur all the way down to the loch side road. From up here you get stupendous views on both sides over Loch Lomond and its islands. I have walked on hills all around Loch Lomond and I doubt if there is a better viewpoint over it than this. The further you descend the more deeply defined the path becomes, until as you start to descend steeply at the end of the ridge it is a red-earth highway of a footpath. Keep on this footpath down through the woods to a stile.

Turn right here and walk along the tarmac road. After about half a mile, as the loch reappears on your left, go left into the car park at Milarrochy Bay. There is a board here displaying the name. As you approach the loch shore go left to pick up the thistle waymarker. Notice the abundance of oak trees as you walk through the woods here. This explains the existence of the factory that used to be in Balmaha. The fact that the factory was there may also explain why Loch Lomondside is so relatively well wooded compared to the rest of the Highlands. When you emerge from the forest go directly forwards, keeping the loch on your near right.

Look out for goosander here. You will probably only see them in silhouette against the water. Look for a long, narrow duck with a drooping fringe behind its head and a long, slim bill which points downwards at its tip. These ducks are members of the sawbill family i.e. they have serrated edges to their bills to enable them to secure struggling slippery fish. These ducks need a steady supply of small fish so their presence on the loch is a marker of a healthy ecosystem.

Further along you come to a fork in the path which is not waymarked. Climb up and away from the loch to your left. At the top move into the open space and enjoy the views over Loch Lomond.

This is Craigie Fort, which controlled the Pass of Balmaha beneath it. This narrow entranceway provided the only land access to the eastern loch side so Rob Roy could drive a herd of stolen cattle through here. He could then leave a few men here to frustrate the efforts of the irate owners of the cows pursuing him.

From the open space on top of Craigie Fort drop down to your right to find the WHW thistle waymarker into Balmaha. Just after this waymarker go straight ahead at an unmarked junction, bypassing the path on your right. At the bottom of the hill go left along the tarmac road. At the junction bear to your right along the pavement into Balmaha. The steep road on your left is the Pass of Balmaha. Passfoot Cottage was a tollhouse. This slope is part of the boundary fault that separates the Highlands from Central Scotland. As every Scottish schoolchild is taught, this Highland Line runs from Helensburgh to Stonehaven. The Oak Tree is up on your right, just past the Highland Way Hotel. This building used to be the chemical factory.

If this walk is not a long enough for you, you can walk down the side of the Oak Tree to MacFarlane's Boatyard and get a ferry to Inchcailloch. This island is a nature reserve and has paths laid out for walkers.

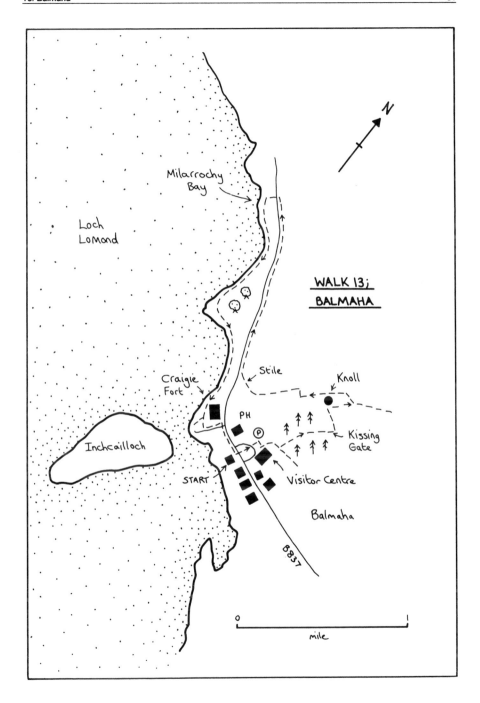

Loch Lomond

Milarrochy Bay

WALK 13; BALMAHA

Stile

Craigie Fort

Knoll

PH

Inchcailloch

Kissing Gate

START

Visitor Centre

Balmaha

B837

0 mile 1

---

14. Rowardennan

Route: Rowardennan – Ben Lomond Path – Blairvockie – Sallochy – Ross Wood

Distance: 5½ miles

Map: OS Landranger 56, Loch Lomond and Inveraray

Start: Rowardennan Hotel, Rowardennan

Access: This walk is not feasible by public transport. In 1998 not even the ferry from Inverbeg was running. By car: Rowardennan is on the eastern side of Loch Lomond, about 25 miles north-west of Glasgow. From Glasgow city centre take the A82 westwards to Anniesland Cross. Here go right on the A739 (switchback) towards Bearsden and Milngavie. After a couple of miles the road splits. The A81 goes right for Milngavie but you should go straight ahead on the A809. About 12 miles along this road a sign directs you left into Drymen. In Drymen village a sign directs you left to Balmaha. About five miles down this road you arrive in Balmaha. Go through the village on this road and follow it around to the right up a steep hill. Keep on this road for the next six miles. There is one unsignposted ambiguous fork, go left here. The Rowardennan Hotel is on your left and is signposted. It has a largish car park. If this is full there is public car parking about 100 metres beyond the hotel.

The Rowardennan Hotel

There has been a drovers' inn at Rowardennan (St Adamnan's Point) since at least 1696. In that year the 3rd Marquis of Montrose acquired a Crown Charter for a howf here. This means 'a place of comfort and good cheer'. In 1696 the howf had a thatched roof. The drovers brought their cattle across the loch by ferry en route to markets such as Drymen.

In 1716 an expedition to punish the MacGregors for one of their many wrongdoings arrived here by ship. They set fire to a few little boats and returned home victorious! Robin Oig, the youngest of Rob Roy's sons, abducted the heiress Jean Key of Edinbelly and made her marry him here in 1750. For this he was hanged in Edinburgh in 1754. The hotel had its own church for the use of its residents. This was once common in remote Highland hostelries. The hotel has a photographic plate of itself at sometime between 1850 and 1860. It was taken by the acclaimed Victorian snapper George Washington Wilson. The hotel remained in the ownership of the Montrose family until 1926.

Since then it has had numerous owners. It was taken over by Peter Jackson, the present owner, in 1995 after he sold his engineering company. It was in a shocking state. He has spent the time since bringing it up to its present excellent standard. There is a long-case clock in the hallway inscribed 'This I'll defend'. This is from the clan crest of the MacFarlanes across the loch.

The bar is modern and comfortable with light wood and pictures of the Highlands. The much larger lounge is like a huge conservatory overlooking the gardens. It has dark wood beams, dried flowers, nice lamps and hanging baskets outside. It is spacious and relaxing. They do ask walkers to enter by the main road, where there is an anteroom for dirty boots, rucksacks and wet clothes. There are only keg beers: Tennents Velvet 70/-, Tennents Lager, Grolsch, Guinness, Caffreys and Dry Blackthorn Cider. There are real fires in the winter. Opening hours are 11.00 to 24.00 Monday to Saturday and 12.00 to 24.00 on Sundays. Interestingly, the gents' loos here have machines that sell Anadin, Bisodol and shaving kit as well as the usual condoms.

There is good selection of home-cooked food. The hotel has a Royal Charter for salmon netting rights in Loch Lomond so this might be something to try. Food is served from 11.00 to 21.30 seven days a week. Children are welcome. Telephone 01360 870 273.

Loch Lomond

This is the largest loch in Scotland. It is 21 miles long and 4 miles wide at its widest, but for much of its length it is a mile or less wide. The surface area is around 27 square miles. It is only nine metres above sea level but is 309 metres deep at its deepest. It has 38 inches (Gaelic for islands).

As befits Scotland's largest loch, Loch Lomond has the largest number of fish species (18) in any Scottish body of freshwater. Notable is the powan, a member of the salmon family. This fish is found in only one other Scottish loch. It is currently under threat from a fish called the ruffe, which is thought to have been introduced by anglers. Although

Loch Lomond

the ruffe is much smaller than the powan it eats its eggs and young. Otters are also making a comeback in Loch Lomond.

People first arrived on the loch shores about 5000BC. These were hunter/gatherers. About 4000BC Neolithic farmers began to cultivate forest clearings. They were followed by the warrior Celtic tribes of the Bronze and Iron Ages. The Romans came and disappeared in a brief space of time. After the fall of the Roman Empire, from the 5th century AD onwards, the Scots from Ireland and their missionaries arrived. One such was Kentigema who lived on the island of Inchcailloch (island of the nuns) just off Balmaha. She died there in AD733. In 1263 the Vikings transported their long ships overland for one and half miles from Arrochar at the head of Loch Long the to Tarbert on the mid-west of the loch. They then ravaged the loch side and island communities. Tarbert in Gaelic means 'portage'. The Scots ruled until the early Middle Ages, when they were gradually replaced by Normans brought in by Scottish royalty for their fighting, organisational and castle-building skills.

Dr Johnson was one of the first to see the tourist potential of Loch Lomond. Other famous or literary figures who were inspired by or wrote about Loch Lomond include Thomas Gray, Dorothy Wordworth,

Keats, Queen Victoria and Tobias Smollett. Smollett, a local boy from the Vale of Leven, called it Scotland's Arcadia.. Another famous figure here was Lady Arran, whose brother was Sir Ivan Colquhoun of Luss. She broke her own world water speed record at the age of 62. She lived on Inchconnan (Colquhouns Island).

The Walk

Leave the Rowardennan Hotel and turn left up the road. Where the road forks go right, and after 50 metres go right again around and behind the public toilets. The path up Ben Lomond is very well travelled and truthfully, unmissable. Ascend this path through the trees.

At the end of the trees and before the footbridge, bear right along the fence at the end of the forest. It is the best part of a mile to here. At the top of the small rise walk diagonally left away from fence and forest to reach a farm gate. Pass through another farm gate about 50 metres beyond the first one. Please leave gates as you find them. Follow the obvious cart track ahead of you down the valley to Blairvockie Farm. This is about a mile and a half ahead of you.

Blairvockie Farm, a 2050-hectare (5125-acre) hill sheep farm includes the summit of Ben Lomond (3460ft/1065m) and is a National Trust for Scotland property. In the spring and early summer look out for the little, yellow, four-petalled flowers of tormentil hugging the ground beside this track. There are good views over Loch Lomond to be enjoyed as you gradually descend. Also keep your eyes open for wild goats as there is a herd on eastern Loch Lomond. They do not survive as well as sheep on the hills as their coats are not as waterproof. Prolonged wet, cold weather periodically depletes their numbers.

After going through a number of farm gates you will arrive at Blairvockie Farm. Go through a gate into the farmyard then turn left at the end of the buildings and follow the tarmac farm road down to the main loch side road. Proceed left along this for about half a mile, going past two entrances on the right to the University Field Centre. Cross a bridge and go immediately right into Queen Elizabeth Forest Park, Sallochy. Walk through the car park almost to the loch and pick up a thistle waymarker for the West Highland Way on your right. Cross a footbridge and follow the waymarkers for about a quarter of a mile. There is some planked walkway along here.

Go left when you reach the rough road just after the boathouse and

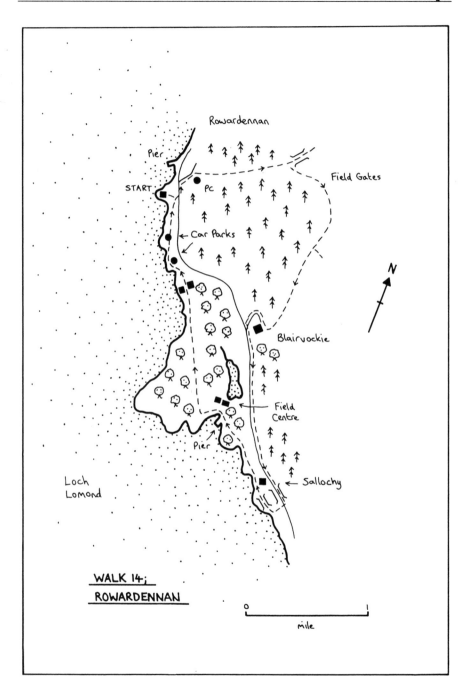

Rowardennan

Pier

START

PC

Field Gates

Car Parks

Blairvockie

Field
Centre

Pier

Loch
Lomond

Sallochy

N

WALK 14;
ROWARDENNAN

0   1

mile

pier. A noticeboard immediately before here gives details of the field station's work. After about 50 metres a thistle waymarker guides right off the rough road and onto a well-made path uphill. There is a seat here for the tired. Stay with this well-made and waymarked path for about a mile, crossing footbridges as and when they appear. When the loch side road appears in front, go left straight away and through the car park by a minor path. At the far side of the car park pick up the waymarked path again. Shortly after this go directly through another small car park to the waymark at the opposite end of it. Approximately 100 metres afterwards follow the waymarkers' guidance left along a rough road. This leads directly on to a path through the trees. It disappears for about 100 metres in this section but just keep the loch on your left and you will soon see the path again. When the path terminates at the main road the thistle waymarker points left. The Rowardennan Hotel is 100 metres on your left up here.

15. Fairlie

Route: Fairlie – Bourtees – Fairlie Glen – Fairlie Castle – Millers Walk

Distance: 3 miles

Map: OS Landranger 63, Firth of Clyde

Start: Village Inn, Fairlie

Access: Fairlie is about 25 miles south-west of Glasgow. It is on the Clyde coast just south of the holiday resort town of Largs. By car: from Glasgow take the M8 westbound towards Glasgow Airport. At junction 28a join the A737, heading for Johnstone. Go down this road for about eight miles. At a roundabout go right on the A760, signed for Lochwinnoch. Go past Lochwinnoch and follow this road until it winds and descends the steep Haylie Brae to the A78 (T) coast road at Largs. At this T-junction turn left for Fairlie. After a couple of miles you come to the start of Fairlie village. There is a church and a large, free-standing Celtic cross on your right. About 20 metres past this on the right is the car park of the Village Inn and Mudhook Restaurant. If this car park is full then double back and go left between the church and Celtic cross. Go left again after about 20 metres and there is a free car park on your left. By train: there is a regular train service from Glasgow to Largs, and Fairlie is on this line. Fairlie Station is also on the route of the walk. For details get a timetable at Central Station, Glasgow or call 0345 484950.

Village Inn

There has been a pub here since 1800 although it has been enlarged since then. As you look at this inn from Bay Street, on the opposite side from the car park, the house on its immediate left was the Fife family home. They used to look out of their windows over the boatyard to check that their workers were not slacking. In those days there were no houses between the inn and the shore. Various members of the Fife family used the facilities of this hostelry. Originally it was a coaching inn serving the coast road.

Inside, the maritime theme is continued. The bar has charts on the walls and the decor includes ships' lamps, ships' crests, pictures of ships, flags and maritime buoy systems. It is a small, dark-panelled bar with blue leatherette seats. It has a fruit machine, darts, TV (including Sky) and a coffeemaker. The comfortable lounge continues the sailing ambience and has a real fire in winter. There is a small beer garden.

The choice of keg beers only is from Millers, McEwans Lager, McEwans 60/- and 80/-, Tartan Special, John Smiths, Guinness and the ubiquitous Strongbow Dry Cider. Opening hours are Monday to Wednesday 11.00 to 24.00, Thursday to Saturday 11.00 to 01.00 and Sunday 12.30 to 24.00.

Landlord Graeme Lavery runs a warm, friendly local. In fact, one of his regulars tells him that if he wins the lottery he will buy the other pub in the village so that Graeme can run this one for him as well. Walkers will receive a friendly reception. There is a good choice of home-cooked, reasonably priced food. A Sunday lunch for two children under the age of ten comes for the price of one. Bar food is served from 12.00 to 14.45 Monday to Friday, 12.00 to 20.45 Saturdays and 12.30 to 20.45 Sundays. There is also the Mudhook restaurant here. Telephone 01475 568 432.

Fairlie

This settlement started as a fishing village. It became mildly famous for its smoked fish. If you have time you could visit Fencebay Fisheries where the smoking is done on the premises. These smoked seafood specialists are two miles south of Fairlie on the A78 (T). Telephone 01475 568 918. Kelburn Country Centre on the edge of this walk has much to do and see for adults and children, ring 01475 568121 for details.

But Fairlie prospered on boat-building, which is strange when you consider its flat, open, unsheltered foreshore and the large differential between high and low tide ranges. Boat-building here is the story of the Fifes of Fairlie dynasty. The Fifes started boat-building here in 1800. Young William Fife built himself a rowing boat (his family were woodworkers) to visit the ships that laid up in Fairlie Bay before going on to Glasgow. He wanted to hear the sailors' stories. This boat was so well built that a ship quickly purchased it. He built another one and the same thing happened again. He quickly realised that he was onto a good thing.

Over the next few generations the Fifes established a shipyard here.

This mainly made sailing boats and, particularly, racing yachts. These were the Rolls-Royces of yachts. Fifes were known for rejecting any wood with knots in it and generally being demanding of the highest quality materials and craftsmanship. One of Sir Thomas Lipton's challengers for the Americas Cup was made here. Fifes also designed another. They also designed a yacht for the King of Spain, which was built in Santander.

Boat-building brought prosperity to Fairlie. In 1800 the population was 132, and there were four carpenters, but by 1841 the population had risen to 521. Five gave their occupation as 'carpenter' and five more as 'boat-builder'. In 1881, out of a population of 720, there were 23 carpenters, six boat-builders and 12 joiners.

Two world wars saw the end of Fifes of Fairlie, but evidence of their presence remains in the village. The steeple of the church by the Village Inn has a model of the *Latifa* as a weathervane. This was a lovely cutter built in 1936 by Fifes. 'Latifa' is a Hebrew word meaning 'beautiful thing'.

The Walk

Leave the Village Inn via its car park. Turn left along the main road for about 200 metres. Just before the garage turn right up the rough road. Climb up the hill with the burn on your right, it is not too steep. At the four-way junction jink slightly right and left to go half left ahead. Do not ascend the steep track into the trees; instead take the less steep road with the fence on its left. From up here you get tremendous views over the Clyde Estuary.

When you arrive at the sign that says Kelburn Country Centre turn right, doubling back on yourself on a rough track through woods. At the end of the woods continue along this track towards the isolated farm of Bourtees ahead. At Bourtrees go through a gate, closing it behind you, and contour walk along the hillside.

At the T-junction at the end of this track go through the solid metal gate and turn right. Walk downhill with the Fairlie Burn on your left and go past ruined Fairlie Castle on your left. If you come here in the spring/summer notice the red campion beside the track. It has five red/pink petals with a bulbous bit behind the flower.

Which you reach the tarmac road go forward and directly downhill. After about 100 metres, as the road bends sharply right, you dog-leg left

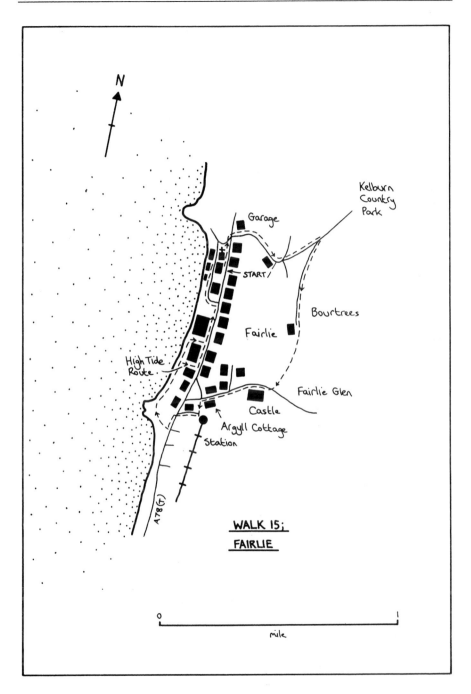

N

Kelburn
Country
Park

Garage

START

Bourtrees

Fairlie

High Tide
Route

Fairlie Glen

Castle

Argyll Cottage

Station

A78(T)

WALK 15;
FAIRLIE

0   1

mile

on a very minor road. When after about 30 metres this very minor road reaches Argyll Cottage it goes hard right. Go straight ahead on the tarmac footpath over the Fairlie Burn. This brings you out at the station, where you turn right downhill towards the main road.

Turn left along the main road. After about 100 metres turn right at the sign for toilets, hairpinning back on yourself. You now walk along the seafront. On your left are the two Cumbrae Islands. Little Cumbrae is to the south of Great Cumbrae. Go straight ahead along the path for pedestrians only, keeping the car park and toilets on your left. Cross the footbridge and proceed down Miller's Walk with the wall on your right and the sea on your left. There are numerous seats along here where you can sit and enjoy the view. Keep along here until the footpath ends at a wall. Here turn right up a narrow entry to the main road.

Fairlie Castle

Note: At higher tides the second half of Miller's Walk can be underwater. If this coincides with your walk, turn right just before the grass ends and follow this nameless little road up to the main road. In both cases turn left along the main road, called, unsurprisingly, Main Road. Then turn left at the Kelburn Hotel into Bay Street. Follow it down and around to the right. The Village Inn is about 100 metres up here on your right.

16. West Kilbride

Route: West Kilbride – Drummilling – Hunterston Sands – Hunterston Power Station – The Three Sisters – Portencross – Seamill

Distance: 7 miles

Map: OS Landranger 63, Firth of Clyde

Start: Inverclyde Hotel, West Kilbride

Access: West Kilbride is approximately 25 miles south-west of Glasgow city centre. By car: take the M8 westwards towards Glasgow Airport. Go off at junction 28a and directly onto the A737 for Johnstone. Follow this road until you reach Dalry. There take the B780 on your right. This road then forks, both of which are the B780. Take the left-hand fork for Ardrossan and West Kilbride. Drive along here for roughly three miles. When the road forks take the right-hand fork, the B781, for West Kilbride. On this road you will pass Blackshaw Farm Park, which is great for children. When you see the sign 'Welcome to West Kilbride' turn left and go along Gateside Street. At the no entry sign bear left as directed by the arrow. Turn right about 30 metres after the telephone box on your right and drive up between the two church steeples. Go through West Kilbride on this road until you hit the main coast road, A78 (T). Turn left here. About 200 metres along here the Inverclyde Hotel is on your right. It has a large car park behind, which you turn into immediately past the hotel.

Inverclyde Hotel

As you enter some pubs the ambience rushes up and shakes you warmly by the hand. In this case it is idiosyncrasy. This pub has an atmosphere of mild eccentricity. Perhaps it is the plastic skull leering from behind the bar with a cigar in its teeth. Well, I hope it is plastic – I never asked. Maybe it is the clocks that run backwards, handy things to have in a pub. Possibly it is the other horological oddities, the beeswax sculptures or the collection of antique blowlamps, but this is definitely a unique pub, one out of the ordinary, a collectors' item.

However, it still gets the basics right. Landlord James Cockburn (pro-

nounced Coburn) and his wife Elaine have 45 years combined experience in the licensed trade behind them, and it shows. Besides the
peculiarities, the bar is beautifully decorated with a tremendous collection of tankards, horse brasses, ships' wheels and pictures. And it is
Ayrshire and Arran Tourist Board approved. Inverclyde means 'mouth
of the Clyde'. The hotel was built in 1907 and was once a temperance
hotel.

It is not now. James Cockburn tells me that he has not the cellars or
demand for real ale. What he serves is Calders Cream and 70/- Ales,
Guinness, Kilkenny, Lowenbrau, Carlsberg Lager and Strongbow Dry
Cider. Opening hours are Sunday 12.30 to 24.00, Monday to Wednesday 11.00 to 24.00 and Thursday to Saturday 11.00 to 01.00. Children
are no problem – in fact, James Cockburn says that it is their parents that
can be the problem.

Food is served all day: it is a hotel. High teas, that grand old Scottish
institution, are available. There is a good selection of reasonably priced,
quality food. The chicken in my sandwich was real chicken, not the re-
constituted, sliced to nothing meat that is so common nowadays. Telephone 01294 823 124.

Hunterston

This peninsula was a notorious haunt of 'Free Traders'. 18th and
19th-century parish records are full of their doings. The smuggling was
controlled from the Isle of Man. Contraband included spirits, tobacco,
lace, spices, salt, tea and coffee. Cargoes were landed in the Portencross
area and hidden in dykes, drains, dung heaps, whin bushes etc. When it
was safe to do so they were carried by horse or even people to Saltcoats,
West Kilbride and Dalry, where they found a ready market. 'Cheap, Sir,
it fell off the back of a boat'. Tea and coffee were much more expensive
then, largely because of duty, and were luxury goods. Sometimes these
'duty-free' items were smuggled in coffins as it was considered unlucky
to see a funeral in those days, and customs officers were as superstitious
as anyone else.

A Mrs Donaldson of West Kilbride had a cask of brandy sitting in the
middle of her kitchen when the Revenue called. Quick-wittedly she
threw a plaid over it and sat on it, nursing her baby and chatting to the
excisemen. Another customs officer was sitting on a barrel of brandy in
a local house when the lady of the house threw the contents of a snuff

The Three Sisters, West Kilbride

box in his eyes. While he blundered blindly around, the evidence of their evasion of duty was spirited away.

Portencross Castle

This was built in 1370. Robert the Bruce signed the charter establishing West Kilbride in an earlier version of this castle. He gave the lands around it to the Boyd family and they stayed here until 1660. At which time they moved into more sheltered accommodation inland. In 1588 a galleon from the Spanish Armada was wrecked here. West Kilbride burgh records of the time record provision being made to feed and clothe the Spanish sailors.

This type of castle had a great hall and kitchen on the first floor, two floors of bedrooms above that and an attic at the top. The upper stories were accessed by a wheel (spiral) staircase. Access to the first floor was by a wooden outside staircase that could be pulled up at the first sign of trouble.

Portencross is unusual in having a second kitchen and entrance on the ground floor. This is because the Stewart Kings, such as Robert II, stayed here while travelling between Dundonald inland and the Isle of

Bute. Soldiers and servants stayed outside under canvas and fed from the ground floor while the nobility feasted from the first-floor kitchen in the great hall.

The Walk

Come out of the Inverclyde Hotel and turn right down the main road. Just opposite Seamill Hydro turn left up Glenbryde Road. When this road forks take the upper (left-hand) fork. At the three-way junction at the top take the central path, where the sign says 'Footpath through Glen to West Kilbride'. Follow this broad, beaten-earth footpath along the left-hand side of the river, bypassing minor paths to left and right. This brings you out at Glen Road. Go straight ahead to the main road and turn right. There are some lovely old buildings here. Walk past the Church of Scotland, St Andrew's and turn left up a lane on the church's right-hand side. At the end of this lane cross the road and go straight ahead up narrow Drummilling Road. Go past the cemetery on your right and its 'Footpath to Kilrusken Road' sign pointing your way. At the end of the road pick your way through the sand and gravel heaps to two kissing gates in line in front of you. Go through these and there are expansive views over the Clyde Estuary. Follow the faint path in front of you to Drummilling House. At Drummilling House go through the left-hand of the two gates. Walk straight ahead and then left between the buildings. Turn right and walk down the cart track to the minor road.

Turn right along this minor road and wander along it for about half a mile. It is not too busy a road. At the main road, cross to the pavement and turn right along it. After about 100 metres turn left between the two stone gateposts. A sign here informs you that Hunterston Castle is one mile ahead. After about two thirds of a mile on this very quiet road you will find a signpost on your left for Goldenberry and Campbelton Farms, go up here.

People with the surname 'Hunter', like myself, might be very interested in what lies ahead at this point: if you go straight ahead here and left at the next junction you arrive at the Clan Hunter Museum. However, it is half a mile off route to the museum and then a further half mile to Hunterston House to pick up the key. The key also has to be returned so in all it can be a diversion of some three miles. So unless you have loads of time and energy, perhaps it would be best to return another time by car.

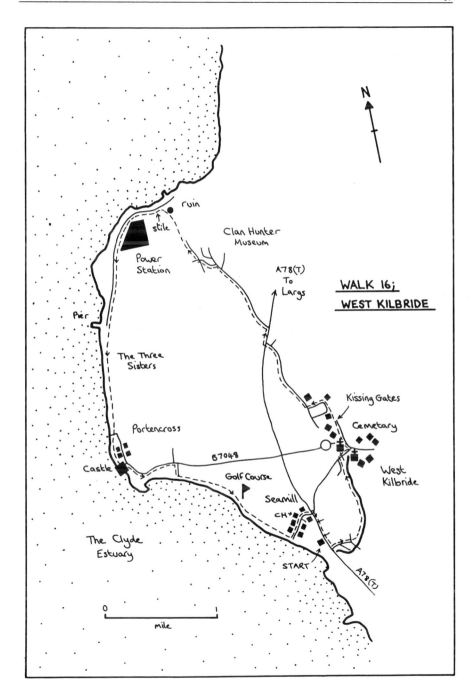

N

ruin
stile
Clan Hunter
Museum
Power
Station
A78(T)
To
Largs

WALK 16;
WEST KILBRIDE

Pier

The Three
Sisters

Kissing Gates
Cemetary

Portencross

B7048

Castle

Golf Course

West
Kilbride

Seamill
CH

The Clyde
Estuary

START

A78(T)

0   1
        mile

Hunterston Power Station is now visible on your left front. The farm road goes round to the right and straightens up to the left. Just after it straightens up go right at the four-way junction, down the cart track. Go through a gate and keep with the cart track as it bears left. At the ruined farmstead go through the gate and turn right. Walk down to the fence and left along it to find a stile. Having crossed the stile walk up the access road to Hunterston Power Station. Look out for oystercatchers and shelduck here.

There is a visitor centre about half a mile up here on your right. There are also guided tours of the power station. For information ring 0345 251251 (local call rate). Tours take a bit of time!

Once past the visitor centre continue on this road to the pier. Where the road ends there is a footpath in front of you. Cross a stile and follow this between the cliffs and the sea. The three parallel crags on your left are the Three Sisters, seabirds nest here. Continue on this path for about a mile until you reach the long-visible Portencross Castle. At Portencross Castle take the lane on your left.

At the end of the lane take the tarmac road to the right. There is a footpath beside this road. When you arrive at Kirkfield House a sign guides you right on a footpath to the shore. Go through a gap on the left of a gate and past the golf course on your left. Then go left on the obvious gravel footpath twixt shore and golf course. Signs here say 'Danger! Golfers at play', so beware of low-flying golf balls.

Walk beside the sea for about a mile. When the path ends turn left up the tarmac road amid houses. Follow this road around to the right past West Kilbride Golf Clubhouse on your left. Then go right at the main road. The Inverclyde Hotel is about 200 metres along on your right.

---

17. Chatelherault
Country Park

Route: Millheugh – Cadzow Ancient Oaks – Cadzow Castle – Chatelherault – Green Bridge

Distance: 5½ miles

Map: OS Landranger 64, Glasgow

Start: The Applebank Inn

Access: Millheugh is on the edge of Larkhall in the valley of the Avon Water, south of Hamilton. This is 17 miles south-east of Glasgow in the orchard country of the Clyde and its tributary the Avon. In the mid-17th century the name Larkhall was shortened from Laverockghaugh, which in Gaelic means the 'lark on the hill'. By car: take the M74 southbound out of Glasgow to junction 7, signposted for Larkhall. Turn right at the T-junction with the A72, marked Larkhall. Immediately across the motorway a sign points left to Larkhall, follow this. In Larkhall go straight through a roundabout and a set of traffic lights. Keep on this road to a T-junction. Here turn right along MacNeil Street. Go down MacNeil St. for about half a mile and turn left at a mini roundabout. The Applebank Inn is about 100 metres up on the left. There is parking at the pub. If the car park is full there is another car park at the mini roundabout. Access to this walk is really only feasible by car as there are no direct bus services from Glasgow to Larkhall. However, you could get a bus or train to Hamilton, walk to Chatelherault (about a mile from central Hamilton) and pick up the walk from there.

The Applebank Inn

This is not a pub for those of a nervous disposition: it is the most haunted pub in Scotland. Till rolls spool out without the till being touched. A table for two is set out in the wee sma hoors when nobody has access to the pub. Two glasses are found in the morning on either end of a stone lintel in the bar that was cleared the night before. This lintel is the key to the haunting. Previously this was the lintel over the entrance to Broomhill House, the family home of the MacNeil Hamiltons

The Applebank Inn

nearby. It was transferred here after Broomhill House was burnt down. As you enter Applebank Inn look left and the lintel is there beside the bar. You can see the coat of arms of the MacNeil Hamiltons on it.

Captain MacNeil Hamilton brought a 'Black Lady' back with him from South Africa in 1902. She was Sita Phurden and originally from Ceylon. In 1904 she disappeared one night and was never seen again. Subsequently a 'Black Lady' haunted the site of Broomhill House, and shortly after the lintel was moved to the pub these odd occurrences began to happen.

But the pub has a history that goes back well before these events. This pub is first recorded in 1714, under the management of 'Big Lizzie'. It was an alehouse serving travellers crossing the river on the ferry that was then here. Later it became an inn when it became legal to sell ale and spirits on the same premises. That would have suited the 'half and a half' drinkers of my Glasgow youth.

To the right of the lintel are bells. In the late 18th century this inn was the property of a Captain Morgan, a former ship captain and these are bells off the ships he served on. The walls of the pub are lined with photographs giving details of local history. It is a treasure trove of information and is well worth spending some time looking at. If you are interested then Cathie Chalmers, the landlady, is the person to talk to. Though she says of the 'Black Lady', 'The only spirits I want to see are those on the gantry behind the bar.' Talking of which, they will mix you a special Black Lady cocktail here. Walkers are warmly welcomed.

The home-cooked food is excellent and there is plenty of choice fare. Booking is recommended if you want to eat here at weekends. Serving hours for food are 12.00 to 14.30 and 18.00 to 20.30 Monday to Friday. On Saturday it is 12.00 to 15.00 and 18.00 to 20.30. On Sundays it is 12.30 to 15.00 and 18.00 to 20.30. Children are allowed in for food in the evenings.

Beer is all keg. Pumps dispense Youngers Tartan Special, John Smiths, McEwans 60/-, Guinness and McEwans lager. Opening hours are 11.00 to 15.00 and 18.30 to 23.30 Monday to Friday. On Saturdays and Sundays the pub is open all day to 23.30, from 11.00 on Saturdays and 12.30 on Sundays. Telephone 01698 884667.

Chatelherault

This name (pronounced 'shattelrow') came from an idea conceived by Anne, third Duchess of Hamilton. Her grandson James, the fifth Duke of Hamilton, carried it out. It is named after a chateau in Poitou. The Hamiltons were made Dukes of Chatelherault by the French king after they assisted him in getting Mary Queen of Scots onto the Scottish Throne. William Adam built it between 1732 and 1744 as a hunting lodge. There was a Grand Avenue of trees connecting this with Hamilton Palace two miles away. If you stand in front of Chatelherault and look north over the Clyde Valley, Hamilton Palace was just to the west of the Mausoleum. The Mausoleum is the large, domed building. From here you may see some of the wild white cattle which are unique to this estate. They differ from the herd at Chillingham in Northumberland in that these have black noses, feet etc. while those at Chillingham have brown.

Chatelherault,s six pavilions had accommodation for hunting staff, kitchens, a banqueting hall and the Duke's private quarters. The courtyard at the rear had kennels, stables, gun and game rooms. The interior was famed for its beautiful ornate plasterwork, the work of Thomas Clayton. There are attractive and extensive gardens that have a Georgian ambience. Alexander Edward originally landscaped the gardens in about 1708.

Chatelherault was damaged by subsidence from mining activity, which is ironic as it was built and paid for by coal. After it came into public ownership it was extensively restored between 1979 and 1987 by Historic Scotland and Hamilton District Council. George Robertson, the local MP who is now Defence Secretary, was heavily involved in this. Entrance is free.

The hunting dog kennels in the rear courtyard have been converted to a modern display. There are exhibitions of local flora, fauna, history of the area and details of Chatelherault. There is also an audio-visual centre with more details of Chatelherault and Tussaud-quality models.

On the death of the 14th Duke of Hamilton, Chatelherault and its estate came into the public domain. The estate was formerly known as Hamilton High Parks and was a hunting reserve. It is now a park of some 220 hectares (550 acres). It is mainly woodland. Some of the woodland in the Avon Gorge is S.S.I. This is because it has been left undisturbed for centuries and is of special scientific value. The Avon Gorge is the main feature of this park. It cuts through the park at up to 725ft (70 metres) deep, exposing strata of sandstone, limestone and coal. If you intend to come here give yourself lots of time. There is much to do and see.

The Walk

Turn left out of the Applebank Inn and walk up to the road bridge. Here continue up the riverbank on the well-defined footpath ahead. This is Morgan's Glen, named after Captain Morgan who had the Applebank Inn in the late 18th century. As the footpath moves away from the river, turn left on another footpath uphill. At the top of the bank go half right towards the end of the viaduct. Turn right onto the viaduct and cross the river. At the far end of the viaduct go left through the bushes and double back on yourself on the tarmac road. The ruins here are those of Broomhill House, beware ghosts and ghouls!

When you reach the road bridge ignore the road on your left and go past this and left onto the tarmac footpath through the bollards. Follow this up the side of the Darngaber Burn and over the Powforth footbridge. Continue uphill and through railings along this tarmac footpath. It eventually becomes a very minor road. Go past the turning on

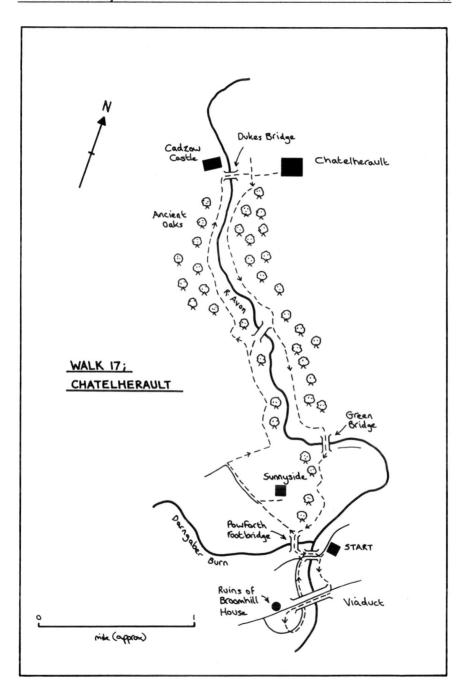

N

Dukes Bridge

Cadzow
Castle

Chatelherault

Ancient
Oaks

R. Avon

WALK 17;
CHATELHERAULT

Green
Bridge

Sunnyside

Darngaber Burn

Powforth
Footbridge

START

Ruins of
Broomhill
House

Viaduct

0   1
mile (approx)

the right hairpinning back to Sunnyside. When this road goes ninety degrees left, turn right along the cart track. At the end of this go through the V-shaped stile into Chatelherault Country Park and turn left along the path. Persevere with this path for the next two miles, ignoring the path down to the right signposted for White Bridge. After about one and a half miles you come to the ancient Cadzow Oaks in a fenced paddock on your left. These ancient trees are said to have been planted in the reign of David I, which makes them at least 800 years old. They look it. With huge trunks and a few spindly branches they have the appearance of African baobab trees or gigantic bonsai.

Immediately after this you will see the Cadzow earthworks on your left, the remains of an Iron Age fort. Shortly after this, take the path on the right signposted Duke's Bridge. From the middle of the bridge you will see the ruins of Cadzow Castle behind you. This was a hunting lodge for David I. This bridge, 27 metres high, was built to link the two halves of the Duke's hunting estate on either side of the valley. Follow the road across the bridge and up the hill. At the T-junction turn right. Take the path on the right through a gate marked for White Bridge.

If you continue on past this path for about 100 metres you will come to Chatelherault House, which you can visit. There is no entrance charge. Keep on the path for a mile approximately. The latter part of this path is the route of an old mineral railway. Keep your eyes peeled for the ruins of Hoolet Row on your left; this was where the miners lived. When I walked along here I found a freshly killed wood pigeon with its head removed and partially plucked, did I disturb a peregrine at its kill? After the eyot (river island) take the path on the left up steps where a sign directs you to Green Bridge. This path soon leads you along the edge of the woods to Green Bridge.

The original Green Bridge has had to be replaced with this current bridge of eki wood. This is a tropical hardwood from sustainable resource forests in West Africa. Follow the path from the far end of the bridge and ignore the tarmac road on your left. About halfway up the hill, at the signpost pointing ahead, take the path on the left going uphill on stairs. This path is not signposted. Continue along this path uphill, then along contours, downhill by a wood and along the riverbank. When this reaches a tarmac path turn left and follow it across the Powforth footbridge then left across the road bridge. Go left at the end of this bridge and the Applebank Inn is about 40 metres along on your right.

18. Lanark

Route: Lanark – New Lanark – Corra Linn – Bonnington Linn – Corehouse – Kirkfieldbank

Distance: 6 miles

Map: OS Landranger 71, Lanark and Upper Nithsdale

Start: Clydesdale Hotel, Lanark

Access: Lanark is in the Clyde Valley about 20 miles south-east of Glasgow. There is a regular train service from Glasgow even on Sundays. However the trains that I travelled on did not have toilets and neither did Lanark Station. Both should have toilets on them. Ring 0345 484950 for times of trains. There are also buses to Lanark. Telephone the Travel Centre on 0141 636 3195. By car: take the M8 eastbound out of Glasgow towards Edinburgh. Go off at junction 8, following signs for Carlisle/The South, to get onto the M74. Leave the M74 at junction 7 and turn left at the T-junction with the A72 for Lanark. Go down the A72 for about 10 miles then turn right onto the A73 at the edge of Lanark. About half a mile further on, almost at the centre of Lanark, you will see the Clydesdale Hotel on your right. The car park is reached by turning right down an unnamed lane immediately before the hotel at Cox's garage. If it is full go up the A706 on the left just before the Clydesdale, signposted to Whitburn. If it is a Sunday you can park on one of the little side roads after you have turned. Otherwise go up here for 100 metres and turn right just before the fire station. There is a large free car park 100 metres along here.

Clydesdale Hotel

This hotel was built on the site of a 14th-century Franciscan friary. The spectre of one of these holy men haunts the basement of the hotel. However he is a friendly friar.

The hotel was erected for the town in 1793 by the Town Council. The councillors were shareholders in this enterprise. It had the first inside water feed and inside toilets in the town. It was a coaching inn. In addition, many buyers, including many from abroad, stayed here as they arranged to purchase the products of New Lanark cotton mills.

Samuel Taylor Coleridge and William and Dorothy Wordsworth stayed here in 1803. There is a plaque outside the hotel commemorating this. Subsequently Charles Dickens stayed here. General Eisenhower is supposed to have stayed here in the Second World War when it was an officers' mess, as it also was in the First World War.

It is not possible to describe the interior as it is being renovated, but the interior and exterior did have an aura of faded grandeur. Gordon Brown, the manager, assures me that walkers will find this a hospitable hostelry. Children are welcome in the lounge but preferably not in the bar.

Food is served from 12.00 to 14.30 and 17.30 to 21.00 Monday to Saturday. Sundays it is from 12.00 to 20.00. There is a good range of traditional bar food. Local produce is used where possible. The exception is seafood as Lanark is quite a way from the sea. All the food is home cooked.

Real ales are Tetley Bitter and Stirling Bitter. Keg beers are Calders Cream Ale, Calders 80/-, Carlsberg Export, Carlsberg Lager, Guinness and there is also Strongbow Dry Cider on draught. The bar is open Monday to Saturday 11.00 to 23.00 and on Sundays 12.00 to 23.00. Telephone 01555 663 455.

Lanark

Lanark is a very old town. The royal castle of Lanark was a residence of David I, 1124-1153, and of William the Lion, 1165-1214. The Scottish Parliament met here between 1293 and 129 5. The castle was occupied by Edward I and Edward II of England but won back in the Wars of Independence.

The Wars of Independence started here. William Wallace killed an English soldier in a quarrel. In retaliation his house was burnt down and his wife killed. Wallace then got together a band of men and attacked the English in Lanark. Wallace killed the English Sheriff Hazelrig with Hazelrig's own sword.

In 1369 Lanark was made one of the four burghs in Scotland responsible for setting standards in weights and measures. Any burgh that wanted standard weights for its markets had to apply to Lanark or one of the other three. Local craftsmen then made these up using the official weights as templates.

On Castle Hill (on the route of this walk) there was a periodic wapinschaw ('weapon show'). The men had to muster with a weapon (sword, spear, battle-axe etc.), a steel breastplate and a steel bonnet. In 1581 it is recorded that only one third of those present were properly equipped. The magistrates were not pleased.

New Lanark

New Lanark

A spinning mill was started here in 1786 by David Dale, known as the Benevolent Magistrate, and Sir Richard Arkwright, the inventor of the spinning frame. Scottish spinning started with local flax in lint mills but by the second half of the 18th century technological innovations such as the spinning frame and Hargreaves' Spinning Jenny made spinning the first large-scale factory business in Scotland.

Arkwright was bought out by David Dale who, with his son- in -law Robert Owen, started the extraordinary social experiment which ended with the present day New Lanark being declared a World Heritage Site. They offered housing to workers who were often immigrants. Indeed, when a storm-damaged ship of Highland emigrants to North America docked at Gourock they inveigled 300 of them to come to New Lanark. They paid workers on occasions when the mills were idle. They established a sick fund. They set up a mill shop where prices were 25 per cent less than the competition and still managed to make £700 a year profit, big money in those days. People used to come from Lanark to here to shop. The shop profits went to pay for the schools they provided. They even supplied a crèche, very modern! And working children continued their education at practically free night classes.

But it was not all philanthropy. The lesson of New Lanark was that a fit and contented workforce is much more productive – they made large profits! As the workforce declined with technological improvements the school was handed over to the Parish School Board in 1875. In 1935 the shop was leased to Lanark Provident Co-op. It was being run as a co-op before this, and paying dividends to its customers.

Subsequently New Lanark's Mills were closed and the site became near derelict. But a community effort resulted in it being restored and opened as a tourist attraction. New Lanark is now thriving again, but in a different line of business.

The Walk

Come out of the Clydesdale Hotel and turn right along the A73. Turn right after about 100 metres at the far end of the church. Notice the large statue of William Wallace on your right on the church front. Go straight ahead after turning right down Castlegate. About 20 metres down here notice the statue of a dog on the roof on your left. Several hundred years ago a Mr MacDonald who lived here suspected Miss Inglis from across the road of poisoning his dog. He had the statue made and erected to stand forever in mute reproach.

Keep descending Castlegate past the Wee Man's pub on your right. This is very attractive part of Old Lanark, which is why it is a conservation area. At the bottom of the hill is Lanark Thistle Bowling Club – directly in front of you on a mound as Castlegate bears right. This was the site of a Roman fort and Lanark Castle. Follow Castlegate right and go left through the archway into Castlebank Park. Go directly ahead on the main track and keep with it as it veers right. Pass the big house on the right.

About 10 metres past this on your left is a sign directing you on the walkway to New Lanark. Take the steps downhill at the plaque giving details of this new walkway. Stay on this broad, well-laid footpath as it zigzags downhill through woodland then go left along the riverbank,

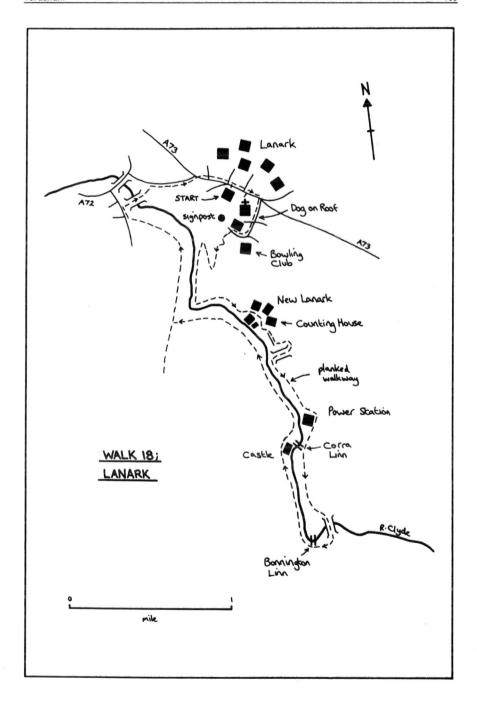

N

A73

Lanark

A72

START

signpost

Dog on Roof

A73

Bowling
Club

New Lanark

Counting House

planked
walkway

Power Station

Castle

Corra
Linn

WALK 18;
LANARK

R. Clyde

Bonnington
Linn

0   1

mile

crossing footbridges over side streams as they occur. This is signposted Clyde Walkway. Just after a footbridge is the first of many fenced viewing platforms on this side of the river. This affords splendid views over the Clyde and New Lanark. After about a mile from Lanark the footpath zigzags briefly uphill to bring you out on a tarmac approach road to New Lanark. Turn right here as the Clyde Walkway sign directs.

There is a lot to see in New Lanark including a Visitor Centre, Mills, Craft Shops, Wildlife Centre etc. So, if you are planing to see sights here it is best to allow an hour or two on your itinerary.

For the walk, go past Robert Owen's House on your right. At the end, where the Village Store is on your left, go to the right of the Counting House and right again down steps. At the foot of the steps go left with the mill lade on your right. At the end of this path go up steps and right across the mill lade. Then take the clear path ahead up steps as it bends left to follow the river. Go through the archway into the Scottish Wildlife Trust's Falls of Clyde Wildlife Reserve. From here a planked walkway and then a beaten-earth path guides you along the riverside. Pass Bonnington Power Station on your right. New Lanark was powered by hydroelectricity at the turn of the century. This was well before the Clyde Valley Electric Power Scheme of the 1920s. There is a signpost here giving details of this power station. Turn right after the power station, guided by a sign for Falls of Clyde. Go with the path and the pipes uphill.

At the top is a viewing platform for Corra Linn. Linn comes from the Gaelic word 'linne' – a 'waterfall'. The river falls 98ft/30m at Corra Linn. The total fall of the river in four miles here is 250ft/77m. From here follow the signs left and right to Bonnington Linn in three-quarters of a mile. It is simply a matter of following the river. In June 1998 there was a peregrine watch here. A pair of falcons was nesting and it was possible to view this for a small charge. If you did not want to see this then you could follow the well-marked and easy to navigate diversion past it.

Once at Bonnington Linn go through the fence and turn right across the Clyde by the footbridge. Then go immediately right again along the dirt track. About 200 metres further on, a footpath on the right leads you along the river bank. Sometimes this footpath can be closed for maintenance but there will be a well-marked and easy to follow diversion. Go past a ruined castle. This is a 15th-century Bannatyne Tower House. This path has yellow waymarkers, be guided by these for the moment. Past Bonnington Power Station this footpath runs directly onto a forest track. At the top of a rise, go directly ahead on the forest track, ignoring the yellow arrow pointing left. There are no more waymarkers. Walk past New Lanark across the river on your right. This track then curves away to the left. At the T-junction turn right. This track eventually becomes a footpath, keep on it for the next mile or so.

You go left off this path and up a bank when the houses come into view ahead. Walk diagonally left on a path at the top of the bank. After about 100 metres you come to a tarmac road. If you go far enough to see the locked gates at the end of this path you have gone too far.

At the tarmac road walk downhill to your right. At the foot of the hill go right across the old bridge before the A72. At the end of the bridge turn right along the A72 for Lanark. Stay on this road. It has a pavement, and a seat approximately halfway up the hill. After half a mile or so you arrive at the Clydesdale Hotel on your right after the junction with the A73.

---

19. Twechar

Route: Twechar – Bar Hill Forts – Croy Hill Roman Fort – Antonine Wall – Forth and Clyde Canal

Distance: 6 miles

Map: OS Landranger 64, Glasgow

Start: The Quarry Inn, Twechar

Access: By car: take the A803 out of Glasgow through Bishopbriggs and towards Kirkintilloch and Kilsyth. As you bypass the northern edge of Kirkintilloch, with the Forth and Clyde Canal on your right, the road veers to the left over the River Kelvin. Just before this bridge take the B8023 to Twechar on your right. About two miles along this road a signpost to Twechar guides you right. Go up here and the Quarry Inn is about 150 metres along on your left. There is parking for about 20 vehicles at the front and side of the pub. By bus: the Kilsyth buses go right past the door of the Quarry Inn. Ask to be put off here. Telephone 01324 613777 for bus details. There is no access by train.

The Quarry Inn

This, unsurprisingly, was a quarrymen's and miners pub in the days when the quarries and mines were open. Miners' Row was just across the road. Landlord Joe Quinn was never happier than when he had a pub full of working men in their dirty boots. It is why the floor is made for easy cleaning. So hikers need have no fear of entering this pub. The miners used to call this pub 'The Bully' and tell their wives, 'Ah'm awa to gie ma money tae the Bully.'

Joe Quinn was one of the first publicans in Scotland to make a feature of real ales. Coachloads of connoisseurs used to come from as far away as Glasgow, Falkirk and Stirling. Joe also used to run real festivals in the pub but he has stopped this now as he has done his 'John the Baptist bit' and caused real ales to be stocked at many other pubs in the locality. Nowadays he runs a cosy, comfortable country pub with a few real ales.

His real ales are Tetley Bitter, MacClays 70/- and MacClays Broad-sword. Sometimes he also has a pump of MacClays 80/-. Non cask-conditioned ales are Tennents lager, Tennents Special and Guinness. There is also Scrumpy Jack cider in the lounge at the back. As well as real ales the pub has a real fire. Opening hours are Monday to Thursday and Saturday 11.00 to 23.30. Friday it is 11.00 to 01.00. Sundays this pub opens 12.30 to 23.00. There is no food but you can bring your own butties as long as you buy something to drink. Telephone 01236 821496.

The Quarry Inn

The Antonine Wall

This was built around AD142 to mark and control the northern frontier of the Roman Empire in Britain. Coins minted in AD142/3 commemo-rate its successful completion. The wall was built by three legions: the II Augustus, the VI Vectris and the XX Valeria Victrix. Each built approximately 13 miles of the wall.

This 39-mile wall stretched between the estuaries of the Forth and Clyde. At various points along the wall were 19 forts at roughly two-mile intervals. The forts at Croy and Bar Hill each had four gates flanked by towers with guard chambers on the lower floors and upper stories linked to the rampart walls. At the centre of the fort was the headquarters or 'Principia'. Other structures included granaries, bath-house, workshops, storerooms, barrack blocks, stables and latrines.

The Antonine Wall was a Murus Cespiticius i.e. a turf structure with a stone base. The base of the wall was about five metres wide, tapering to about two metres wide at the top. It was about three metres high. There was a ditch about twelve metres wide and about four metres deep in front of it on the north side. On the south side of the wall was a Ro-man road about five metres wide that serviced the wall forts. This road was cambered to allow the water to drain off. At this time the Kelvin Valley was an additional boggy moat in front of the wall. The wall was abandoned in AD168/9.

The Forth and Clyde Canal

This was built between 1768 and 1790. It was opened on the 8th of July 1790. It is 20 metres wide, 9 metres deep, and at its highest point is 162ft/50m above sea level. The canal was closed in 1963. In the 1970s a campaign began to reopen it. After repairs by the British Waterways Board and local authorities pleasure boats now run on some sections.

Horse-drawn boats known as swifts operated along the canal. These boats changed horses at set stations along the canal, rather like the Pony Express. Swifts could go from Glasgow to Camelon, where this canal joins the Union Canal to Edinburgh, in three hours. This is a distance of 25 miles.

Puffers also traversed the Forth and Clyde Canal. They were called puffers as the exhaust was turned up through the funnel, producing the characteristic puffing noise that gave them their name. Puffers used derricks to swing a man onto the towpath so that he could run ahead and open locks and bridges. Other boats kept a bicycle aboard for the same purpose. The most famous puffer of all was that used as the *Vital Spark* in the BBC series 'Para Handy'. This was the *Saxon* and it was built by J. and J. Hay at Kirkintilloch, a couple of miles down the canal towards Glasgow.

The Walk

Come out of the Quarry Inn and turn right along the road. After about 20 metres, just before the War memorial, an ancient monument sign points you right uphill to the Antonine Wall and Bar Hill. Follow this cart track around to the right. At the top of the hill turn left through a kissing gate where the concrete dome structure is on your right. Go through another kissing gate and follow the grassy track as it hugs the fence on your right. On your left are the remains of the Roman fort at Bar Hill.

Among the troops stationed at Bar Hill were the first cohort (about a tenth of a legion, 600 men) of the Baestasii from the Lower Rhineland and the first cohort of the Hamii, who were Syrian archers. There was a shrine to the god Sylvanus here. The remains of the headquarters and bathhouse can be seen.

At the end of the grassy track, turn left at the concrete hut, keeping the tumbledown dyke on your right. Go through the dyke towards the plaque giving details of the Iron Age hill fort and past it to the trig point on top of the hill. From the trig point descend the right-hand of the two rides through the forest to find the cart track at its far end. Follow this through the wood. At the end of the wood go through the kissing gate to the right of a farm gate. Keep on this track and go through another kissing gate where a pallet functions as the gate. Turn right at the end of the dirt road onto the B802. A sign indicates half a mile to Bar Hill and the Antonine Wall.

About 100 metres up here go left at the sign 'Croy B802'. In Croy village turn second left after the Celtic Bar then bear right. At the T-junction turn left uphill. The tarmac path is on your right at the top of the hill. When I was there it had gates across it which were partly locked but it was easy enough to get through. If it is securely locked then double back and go up the road beside the Celtic Bar. There are signs to the Roman remains, Croy Hill, which you follow.

This is the only place in Lanarkshire where great crested newts breed. Tarmac, who quarry here, have recently excavated a new pond for them and have renovated some of the existing ones.

From the end of the tarmac path go straight ahead uphill. This is a grass path under telegraph poles. It then bears slightly left. From the top of the hill follow the obvious path to the hill which is most to the left of the three hills directly ahead. Then go straight ahead and follow the path right through a ruined drystone dyke and left along the dyke. Just after a lochan (small loch) on your left you will come to a farm track.

About 50 metres up to your right on this track are the remains of Croy Hill Fort on the Antonine Wall. This fort had a shrine to the Nymphs in it. Go across the farm track and walk down the grassy path, keeping the

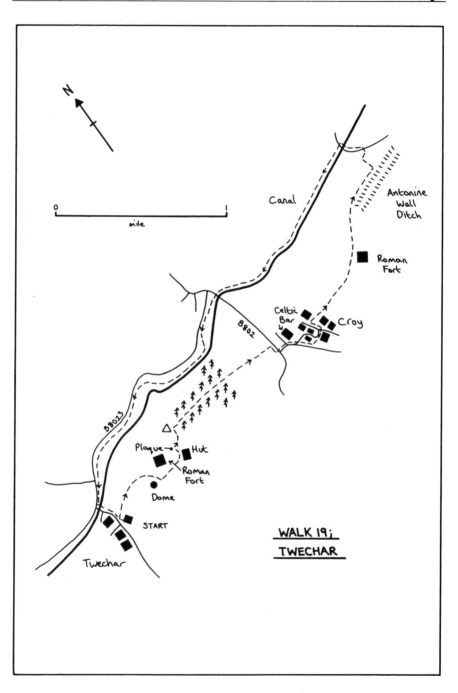

ditch of the Antonine Wall on your right. Follow the course of the wall downhill until you reach a cart track on an embankment cutting across your path. Turn left along this and keep on it as it bears right to reach a tarmac road. Go through or over the gate and turn left down the road to reach the canal visible in front of you.

When the bog was drained here to make the Forth and Clyde Canal, bodies were found from the Battle of Kilsyth nearby. These included a trooper still sitting on his horse. The drainage disrupted the lives of the local amphibians who decamped in search of fresh places to live. This caused a plague of frogs of biblical proportions.

Cross the bridge and turn left along the canal towpath. There is an information board about the canal on your right after you cross the bridge. Follow the towpath for the next two and a quarter miles, staying on this side of the canal. Go under one road across the canal and at the next road you will see a signpost guiding you left to Twechar. About 150 metres up here on your left is the Quarry Inn.

20. Torrance

Route: Torrance – Upper Carlestoun – Muir Head – Lennox Forest – Blairskaith – Balgrochan

Distance: 6 miles

Map: OS Landranger 64, Glasgow

Start: Wheatsheaf Inn, Torrance

Access: The easiest way to get here, by far, is by car. Take the A803 out of Glasgow. Once past Bishopbriggs and into the countryside, go left at the first roundabout and onto the A807 signposted for Torrance. At the Kelvinbridge roundabout at the edge of Torrance take the B822 for Lennoxtown. The Wheatsheaf is about 100 metres up on your right. This pub has a car park. By bus: Henderson Travel runs a spasmodic service to Torrance. For details telephone 0141 635 3195. Note that this bus departs from the western end of Cadogan Street, not Buchanan Street Bus Station.

Wheatsheaf Inn

This pub dates back to 1890. From then until 1976 it was in the hands of the XXX family. Now the Laughlin family runs it and landlord John Laughlin extends the hand of hospitality to all hikers. This pub is used to recreational travellers as it used to be a popular pub with cyclists from Glasgow and was known as the Cyclists' Rest. Even now a motorcycle club meets one evening a week here. However, John Laughlin assures me that they are very well behaved and travel home by taxi.

Not everyone travelled so far to get to the pub. Once a Congregational church held its services on the top floor of the building. I feel that their devotions would have been well attended. And, indeed, the interior of the pub is divine. Old mirrors and leaded glass from previous incarnations of this pub are extensively used as decoration pieces. There is also lots of dark wood including tables and beams. It is a lovely little pub outside and in.

There are fruit machines and a dartboard, and a beer garden. This was the first pub in the West of Scotland to have a beer garden and until just before the Second World War this was an isolated country pub surrounded by fields. The cellars and kitchens have just been renovated. The food is all fresh and cooked on the premises, except for the chips, which are frozen. The food is excellent and there is plenty to choose from. Food is served from 11.00 to 21.30 Monday to Saturday and from 12.30 to 21.30 on Sundays.

There is also plenty of drink to choose from. Cask-conditioned ales are McEwans 80/-, Theakstons Old Peculiar and Belhaven 70/-. On keg are McEwans 70/-, McEwans Lager, Youngers Tartan Special, John Smiths, Heineken, Guinness and Murphys. The pub is open from 11.00 to 24.00 Monday to Thursday and Saturday. Fridays it opens from 11.00 to 01.00 and on Sundays from 12.30 until 24.00. Telephone 01360 620374.

The Wheatsheaf Inn

The Eleven Ploughlands of Balgrochan

This walk takes place in the area anciently known as the Ploughlands of Balgrochan. Some of the names of these Ploughlands still occur on to-day's maps: Carlestoun, Longshot and Newlands. In this vicinity deeply cut burn beds reveal mineral strata on their banks. Sometimes the minerals are even visible on the bed of the burn.

This area has extensive mineral workings so keep to the paths. In 1775 a horse and rider (the rider still having his feet in the stirrups) were discovered at the bottom of a shaft of a coal pit at Bardowie. This is about two miles east of Balgrochan. The body is believed to have been that of a fleeing Jacobite from the 1745 rebellion.

The main minerals worked were coal and limestone but ironstone, fireclay and alum were also mined. Fireclay is heat-resistant and was used for stoves, ovens etc. Sandstone and whinstone were quarried. Mining began here in the 17th century, with the Ploughlands supplying coal to Mugdock and Buchanan to the west of here. Limestone was discovered as a fertiliser in the 1500s, and by the 1700s limestone was also being mined here. There is a story that Glasgow Cathedral is made of local limestone.

The Ploughlairds of Balgrochan would have been farmer/miners at this time. The demands of the farm would have taken first place and mining would only have been possible in the summer (dry season) as this was before the advent of modern drainage techniques. Summer is a busy season on farms so most minerals produced would have been for local consumption, coal for the farm fireplace and limestone for farm field fertilisation. A small surplus would have been exported outside the area. Some lime was exported to Glasgow. In 1767 one of those involved in transporting lime, Lime Jenny, was drowned while trying to cross the Glazert Water in spate with her horse and cart.

By 1800 this was a thriving industry and ironstone was beginning to be mined to satisfy the demand for iron created by the Industrial Revolution. One Glasgow ironmaster with an interest in the area was William Dixon, whose Glasgow ironworks was called Dixon's Blazes.

Alum was also being mined at this point. Alum was needed after Charles MacIntosh (of rubber mackintosh fame) discovered that acetate of alumina could be used to make vegetable dyes fast. With nearby Glasgow and Paisley as major weaving and thus dyeing areas the demand for alum surged. The alum industry declined and died in the late 19th century. Its demise was the result of the easy availability of low-priced sulphuric acid, which could be used with aluminious clay to make alum.

By 1881 all mining had ceased in the Ploughlands of Balgrochan due to extreme exploitation, accumulated waste, damage to farmland and extensive faulting of the strata being mined. Today all that remains are the beds of the old coal roads and the railway lines that make up some of the roads and footpaths of the area.

In the later years of the industry Balgrochan coal and limestone were transported to Glasgow on the Forth and Clyde Canal just south of Torrance. In the early decades of the 19th century the trade was at its peak and producing about 20,000 tons of coal and 2600 chalders of lime per annum. A chalder is 288 gallons.

The Walk

Turn right out of the Wheatsheaf and walk up into the village of Torrance. Just after the Village Inn on your right, on your left is a memorial and inscription to David Ferrie of Balgrochan. When the main road bends right at the Torrance Convenience Store go straight ahead. Turn quickly right up School Road at the Torrance Church of Scotland.

Follow this past the public footpath sign to Acre Valley Road then go sharp left and right around the row of cottages. Ascend the green track up the hill. At the end of the green lane turn left onto the farm track. Continue on this as it bends left past a wood on your left until it intersects with a tarmac road. Turn right up the tarmac road. Just over a burn you come to a sign for Upper Carlestoun Farm straight ahead.

There was once a pit here. The track to your left goes to Langshot Farm and just beyond the farm there were once a pit, a quarry and a fire-clay mine. It seems hard to believe in today's peaceful countryside.

Proceed directly forward almost to Upper Carlestoun Farm. Just before the farm go left through a kissing gate at the sign 'Public Footpath to Lennoxtown'. Come here in March and you may well see the yellow flowers of coltsfoot. It is so called because the leaves are shaped like colts' feet. This path is fenced in. Go through three more kissing gates and then follow the path half right towards the edge of a field.

Now cross the sleeper footbridge and bear left on the obvious path through the woods. Quickly cross a stile with a yellow arrow waymarker and go through the woods with the burn on your left. You may hear the harsh screeching of jays as you walk through the wood, but you are unlikely to see these very shy birds. Jays have a prominent white rump in flight.

Go through a kissing gate at the end of the woods and directly up the field with the hedge on your left, as guided by the yellow arrow waymarker. At the end of the field go straight ahead into a green lane

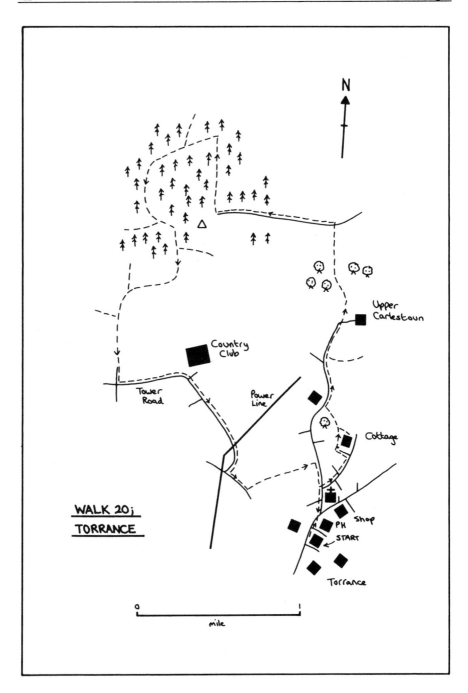

N

Upper
Carlestoun

Country
Club

Tower
Road

Power
Line

Cottage

WALK 20;
TORRANCE

Shop

PH

START

Torrance

0   1

mile

then go through a kissing gate and down a farm track to a T-junction with a tarmac road. Here a signpost points right for Lennoxtown, but you turn left along the tarmac road.

Go into the pine forest along this road. A sign tells you that you are entering Aberfoyle Forest District, Lennox Forest. At the end of the clearing on your left that has a transmitter mast in it there is a 'No Through Road' sign and a pole barrier. At this, just before the track to the transmitter goes off on your left, is a sign on your right for the forest walk. This is your path.

Go along this path, ignoring a grassy path on the right, until you come to a T-junction. Here go left. Keep with this path for the next mile as it bends left and left again until you have reversed your direction of travel. Take the third path on the right downhill. You will see skyscrapers on the horizon at this point. Cross the stile at the bottom of the wood and bear gently right on the farm track.

There are lovely views over the Kelvin Valley from here. After about a quarter of a mile, having passed a cart track joining from the right, cross a stile and go straight ahead downhill. There is another cart track on the right at the stile but vehicular access is blocked off. At the foot of the hill, go directly ahead on the tarmac road. After about 100 metres you come to a four-way junction, turn left here. This is Tower Road. Go past the road to Oscar's Country Club on your left as the road bends right. Continue along Tower Road for about a quarter of a mile. About 200 metres after it bends sharply left under pylons you will find a footpath sign on your left for West Balgrochan.

About 100 metres along this footpath follow the yellow arrow waymarker down the steps, across a footbridge, through the kissing gate and right uphill. Then cross a sleeper bridge and go left uphill. You reach a lane and proceed directly ahead down it. As you arrive here notice the lintel over the door of the house on your left – 'W.M. A.T. 1796'. This is a marriage lintel. When a couple set up home, they put up an inscribed lintel like this over the door. The W.M. stands for William Maitland and 1796 is the year of the marriage. Sir George Pirie, one of the Glasgow boys of the Charles Rennie Macintosh school stayed here at the turn of the century.

The lane ends at a T-junction with a tarmac road. At this point, turn right downhill. At the T-junction at the bottom of the hill turn right and the Wheatsheaf is 200 metres along on your left.

21. Kilbarchan

Route: Kilbarchan – Dampton Pad – Burntshields – Drygate – Kibbleston – Abbanoy – Tandlehill

Distance: 5 miles

Map: OS Landranger 63, Firth of Clyde, and OS Landranger 64, Glasgow

Start: Trust Inn, Kilbarchan

Access: Kilbarchan has no railway station but there are plenty of buses from Glasgow – timetable enquiries: the Travel Centre 0141 636 3195 or Clydeside Buses 0141 885 4040. If travelling by car take the M8 westbound from Glasgow. At junction 28a take the A737 for Dalry. About three miles along here there are signs to Kilbarchan on your left. There is a double roundabout here, go right at the first roundabout and left at the second one. The Trust Inn is about half a mile along on the left. This pub has no car park but street parking is unrestricted as long as you do not park on the pavement. The locals park on the pavement, but you take a risk if you do so.

The Trust Inn, Kilbarchan

This pub was opened by Sir Thomas Glen-Coates, in June 1904. The name Trust Inn does not refer as you might suppose to the nearby National Trust property of the Weaver's Cottage but to the Public House Trust. These government-owned and -run bodies were set up to provide decent quality drinking places for people. This pub was built by the Renfrewshire Public House Trust at a cost, including the land, of about £1000. Their pubs were marked with a yellow star. The star is still on the pub sign outside but painted black now. Here, as well as alcohol, people would be served with tea, coffee and cocoa. It had a tearoom and family section as well as a licensed bar. This pub replaced a shebeen, The Ship, that was just across the road. Some of the stained glass windows from this can be seen from the main road on the outside of this pub.

The Trust Inn has an attractive exterior in kiln brick and roughcast with Victorian windows. The interior is attractively furbished with pictures of old Kilbarchan, horse brasses, brass plates and dark wood beams. Fruit machines and a general knowledge test machine are in the bar.

Mine hosts, Kevan and Barbara Webster, extend the hand of hospitality to weary walkers. Cask-conditioned ales are Deuchars IPA, Tetleys and Burton Ale. Sometimes there is a guest ale. On occasions this pub has beer festivals with up to seven or eight real ales on offer. Keg pumps produce Calders 80/-, Dry Blackthorn Cider, Carlsberg Lager, Calders Cream Ale, Guinness, Tetley Bitter and Stella Artois. This pub is open Monday, Tuesday and Wednesday 11.30 to 14.30 and 17.00 to 23.30. On Thursdays the opening hours are 11.30 until 24.00. Fridays and Saturdays it is open from 11.30 to 00.30 and on Sundays from 12.30 until 23.00.

A good choice of good food is available and all main courses are one very reasonable price. Food is served from 12.00 to 14.00 and again from 17.00 until 21.00. After the kitchen closes, hot boxes are available i.e. hot food in a box such as fish and chips, sausage and chips etc. There is no food on Sundays. Telephone 01505 704828.

Kilbarchan

Kilbarchan is a very picturesque little village. The name means 'the cell of St Barchan', a 6th-century Irish missionary. Later there was a chapel of St Catherine here. The village was founded on this chapel circa 1483 and the chapel was given to the village by Thomas Crauford of Auchames, to the west of the village. The ruins of the chapel are visible in the old churchyard. At this time around forty families employed in farming would have lived here.

In 1317 Marjory, daughter of Robert the Bruce, was badly injured in a hunting accident near Kilbarchan. After dying in Paisley Abbey she was posthumously delivered of a son by caesarean section. This boy became King Robert 11, the first of the Stewart dynasty.

Kilbarchan developed gradually into a weaving village and by 1775 there were some 300 families in the village. The steeple was erected in 1775 by the local laird, a Major Milliken. On the steeple is a statue of Habbie Simpson, the piper of Kilbarchan made famous by the local poet Robert Semple of Beltrees. Habbie was adored for his ability to make people laugh as well as for his piping skills. To this day those born in the parish of Kilbarchan are called 'Habbies'. The wee cottages are mainly 18th century while the houses are mostly 19th century.

Weaving in Kilbarchan was a cottage industry, unlike nearby Paisley. Weaving was done on handlooms rather than on industrial jacquard looms. At its peak in 1830 there were about 800 looms, mainly handlooms, in Kilbarchan.

A speciality of Kilbarchan were 'holey ponchos', which were exported to Mexico and the USA This is the serape that Clint Eastwood wears in the spaghetti westerns. So the next time that you see 'The Man with No Name', think of Kilbarchan.

The Weaver's Cottage contains a working loom and a display of the various tools of the weaver's trade. It also depicts what life would have been like here in olden days. It has displays of domestic implements from bygone times, illustrations of how cooking was done over open fires and typical furniture of the era. The cottage dates from 1723 and the names of the original builders are engraved on the lintel above the front door. In 1801 the cottage came into the possession of William Christie whose family lived and worked here until the 1940s. Look out for the collection of local teapots, one of which has the name Mrs Christie on it, a descendant of the original William Christie.

The Weaver's Cottage is a National Trust for Scotland property. Its opening hours are 5th April to 31st May and 1st September to 1st October, Tuesday, Thursday, Saturday and Sunday 14.00 to 17.00. 1st June to 31st August, open daily 14.00 to 17.00. To double-check the above phone the National Trust for Scotland on 0131 226 5922

The Walk

Turn left as you come out of the Trust Inn and go up the main road, past the war memorial on your left and the bus shelter on your right. Where the main road veers left go straight ahead up Ewing Street. At the top of the hill on your right is the old steeple with the statue of Habbie Simpson on it. A plaque on the church door gives some details about it. Continue down this road for about 50 metres and you will see the Weaver's Cottage on your left at a four-way junction. Go straight ahead here up Shuttle Street. Just before the sign that says Kilbarchan, go left along a minor road. After about 600 metres you will see a sign on your left indicating a public footpath to Dampton Pad, follow this. About 50 metres up this farm track a similar signpost on your right just before a barn takes you into the fields. Go through two fields, keeping the fence/hedge on your immediate left.

Once over the footbridge turn right. Walk beside the burn for about 20 metres, then turn left uphill between the gorse clumps. About 150

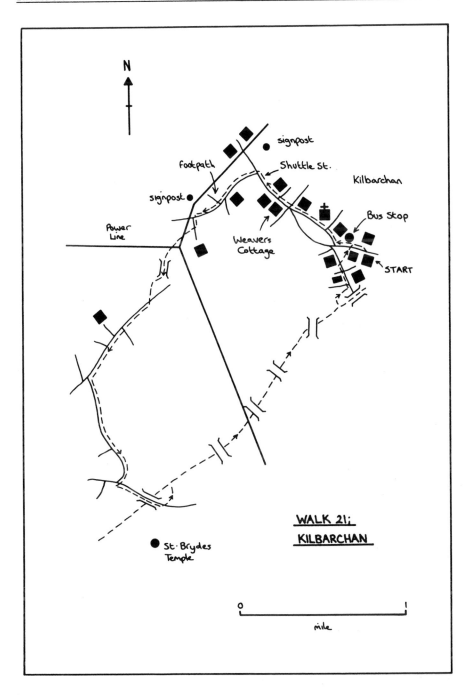

N

signpost

footpath

Shuttle St.

Kilbarchan

signpost

Weavers Cottage

Bus Stop

Power Line

START

WALK 21;
KILBARCHAN

St· Brydes Temple

0   1

mile

metres up here cross the stone step stile in the wall. Cross the field ahead to another stone step stile underneath the footpath sign. Turn right along the road here. As you walk along here Kilbirnie Loch and Barr Loch come into sight ahead. Follow this road under the pylons until you come to a junction on the left, which is followed immediately by one on the right. Go left down here into the valley of the Black Cart Water. At the bottom of the hill the road bends right and terminates in a T-junction, go left here. On your right on a hilltop is the Temple of St Bryde. The Semples, local landowners, built this as a hunt viewing point.

After about 200 metres you will cross a bridge over a railway path. Just past the bridge on your left a path takes you down to the former track. At the bottom go straight ahead on the railway path. Follow it along under four bridges and about 300 metres after the last bridge you will come to a bridge **over** a burn. About 50 metres before this turn left and walk down a path between fences parallel to the railway path. At the foot of this turn left, go along the road for about 100 metres then turn right, just before the substation, over a footbridge onto an enclosed path. This terminates at the main road. Turn right here to return to the Trust Inn, about 100 metres along.

Weaver's cottage, Kilbarchan

22. Lochwinnoch

Route: Lochwinnoch – Low Semple – Howwood – Belltrees – Barcraig Reservoir – Brownmuir – Auchengowan – Auchengrange

Distance: 8½ miles

Map: OS Landranger 63, Firth of Clyde area

Start: The Brown Bull, Lochwinnoch

Access: Lochwinnoch is about 15 miles south-west of Glasgow. For easy access by car take the M8 west out of Glasgow towards Glasgow Airport. Turn off at junction 28a on the A737 towards Johnstone. Follow this down for about eight miles before going right on the A760 to Lochwinnoch at a roundabout. Go between the lochs and under a bridge for about a mile. Turn right where a signpost points to Lochwinnoch/Kilmalcolm B768. This is Main Street. The Brown Bull is about 100 metres up on your right. It has no car park but car parking is unrestricted here. There are regular train services from Glasgow to Lochwinnoch. The railway station is on the route of the walk. Timetables are available from the Travel Centre, St Enoch's Sq. and Central Station, Glasgow. Alternatively, telephone 0345 484950 (local call rates). Check the timetable carefully as not all the trains on this line stop at Lochwinnoch.

Brown Bull

If this pub were a bloke he would be the legendary diamond geezer. Stepping through the door is like stepping back in time. When some work was being done on the walls the old stone walls were found hidden underneath. They are one or two hundred years old. These were exposed and renovated. The result is a pub interior authentic enough to have been a location shot for television's Dr Finlay. Add to this the fact that landlord Jim McKeon can have up to ten real ales on at times and you can see why I am raving about this pub.

The pub dates back to at least 1809. There is a licence for this pub for that year behind the bar. It used to be a coaching inn. Customers stayed next door and used the inn for food and drink. There were two cellars under the building for horses etc. and grooms and coachmen had their quarters at the back of the present pub. Astonishingly, for a place the size of Lochwinnoch, there were once 37 pubs here.

The name Brown Bull is thought to have originated from a Mr Brown, a previous owner. There is a picture of him on a wall of the pub. There are also pictures by local artists adorning the bar walls. Other decor includes oak beams, a 1930s telephone and hop vines on the gantry. Lots of local walkers already use this pub so it is geared up to readily receive ramblers.

Jim McKeon keeps good ale. There are two resident real ales: Orkney Dark Island and Belhaven IPA Also there are two guest real ales which were Belhavens 60/- and St Andrew's when I was there. I arrived at the fag end of a real ale festival, when another six real ales had been on including Schiehallion, Fullers London Pride and Independence from Invergordon. On keg are Tennents Lager, Belhaven Best and Light, Guinness and Dry Blackthorn Cider. Opening hours are Monday to Thursday 12.00 to 23.00, Friday and Saturday 11.00 to 24.00 and Sunday 12.30 to 23.00.

There is no food but if you want to buy a sandwich or something from the local baker's and eat it with your drink that is no problem here. Telephone 01505 843 250.

Lochwinnoch

This village was formed around its chapel. By the beginning of the 13th century this chapel was under the control of Paisley Abbey. The monks taught weaving to the people of the area and this teaching and weaving is illustrated by a couple of ecclesiastical curiosities in the area.

In Lochwinnoch Churchyard there is the Dumb Proctor. This is a carved stone that once had writing on it, but time has worn this to illegibility. Figures of a serpent and of a man riding an ass can still be made out. This was once a teaching aid to preachers. The carvings refer to scenes from the Bible and the divine giving the sermon would use the Dumb Proctor carvings to illustrate his discourse. This was in the days when few people could read or had Bibles. In 1782 this stood at Calderheugh, just on the left as the walk crosses the River Calder on its return to Lochwinnoch.

Auld Simon is the gable-end of a parish church built in 1729. Its weather vane is a plough, while an arrow points north and a rose, a thistle and a shamrock mark the other stations of the compass. The clock and bell in the church helped the weavers organise their day's work so when it was due to be demolished, this gable-end with clock and bell was left standing. Auld Simon is believed to have been one of the weavers whose duties included winding up and maintaining the clock.

Lochwinnoch is also famous for its chairs. Although some of these chairs went for home consumption, many more went into Clyde-built ocean-going liners. Lochwinnoch chairs went into the Lusitania, The Queen Mary and the Queen Elizabeth. One Lochwinnoch firm, Hamilton and Crawford, made chairs which sank with the Titanic in 1912. This firm did so well that it was nicknamed the Klondyke.

Lochwinnoch also has Scotland's 'Bermuda Triangle'. The hills to the north-west of the village in Muirshiel Country Park rise to over 2275ft/700 metres and seem to summon planes to doom. Since 1938 over 20 planes have crashed or been forced down here, often with fatal consequences. Planes that have crashed here include a Wellington bomber on a secret mission in 1941. Its wreckage was blown up and buried. In 1942 a Swordfish crashed and three others had to crash-land as they had run out of fuel. It sounds remarkably like some of the Bermuda Triangle stories. Suggestions as to the cause of this include minerals in the mountains affecting compasses and/or other instruments, or storms in the deeply and steeply plunging glens affecting air currents.

Auld Simon, Lochwinnoch

The Walk

Turn right out of the Brown Bull and walk up the main road. At the top of the hill, where a minor road forks off to the right and the main road goes left, is Auld Simon. Twenty metres before this there is a minor road going off to the right at right angles. This has a brown sign pointing down it to the Visitor Centre. Go down here.

Go under the triple-arched railway bridge and turn immediately left after this and up the ramp to the disused railway line path. Go straight ahead on the railway path at the top, keeping Lochwinnoch village at your back. Go along here for about a mile. Just before the second bridge over the track notice the ruins of the collegiate church on your left.

A collegiate church is a foundation established to say masses for the souls of the deceased members of a family in perpetuity. The family in this case were the Lords Sempill, the first of whom and the founder of this church was one of the 'Floo'ers o'the Forest who fell on Flodden's field. This church was also one of Scotland's first schools. Two singing boys helped the reverend gentlemen in their duties. In return the boys were taught music and grammar. A notice board here gives details of the ornate bridge over a road just ahead. Look out also for the arched stone-work at Low Semple Farm on your right, also mentioned on the notice board.

After about another 400 metres further along the railway line you come to a third bridge over the path. Go under this and about 50 metres beyond on your right double back up the ramp to the road. Turn left down this road. St Bryde's Temple is on its hilltop to your right here. This was a hunting lodge/hunt viewing point for the Sempill family, local landowners.

Walk down this road over the Black Cart Water, the main road and railway and into the village of Howwood. Where the road forks go briefly right to the slanted T-junction and right again. Walk up past Elliston Farm on your left. Just before this road bends right to rejoin the main road there is a very minor road on your left hairpinning back. Go up this road. Go past a drive on your left and about 100 metres before the white house at the top of the hill there is a well-formed footpath on your right.

Go along this footpath, crossing the burn by stepping-stones. Then follow it uphill to a gate. Close the gate behind you and proceed ahead along a cart track bordered by hedges, dykes and fences. At Earlshill on your left go directly forward on the minor road. When this reaches the

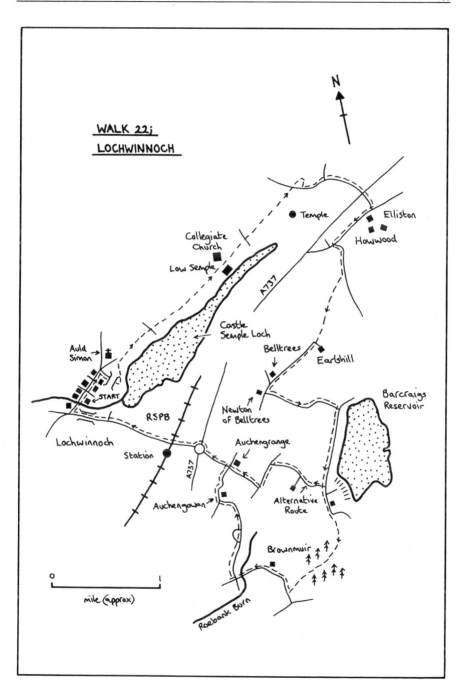

T-junction at Belltrees Farm, bear left. After about 100 metres, at the sign that says 'Hamlet of Newton Belltrees', turn left uphill. Follow this up the gentle slope until Barcraigs Reservoir comes into view. At the T-junction here turn right. Go along here and past the dam on your left. About 100 metres beyond the dam there is a T-junction.

If the weather is foul or you are running out of time you can cut the walk short by turning right here. Then you follow the road down to a T-junction and turn left. At the next junction, at Auchengrange, you turn right. At the main road you go straight across the roundabout and down the A760 into Lochwinnoch, turning right into Main St. where the sign says Lochwinnoch, Kilmacolm B768. Do not cut the walk short here unless you have to as you will miss a lovely hidden valley.

If proceeding with the walk, turn left at the T-junction beyond the dam. Follow the road around to the right as a dirt road goes off left in the direction of the dam. Go through a small valley with an isolated house on your left. At the top, where the road breaks sharply left, go directly ahead up the obvious footpath. Follow this through the woods. It is fenced and dyked on both sides. After the woods keep along the hillside on what is now a cart track for about half a mile, ignoring two tracks off to the right.

At the minor road turn right and follow it around Brownmuir Farm. Just after the road crosses the Roebank Burn, turn right at the T-junction. Follow this along the hillside until it turns left to a T-junction at Auchengowan. Turn right here, being careful of traffic as it is a hidden junction.

When you come to the white wall of Auchengrange on your right, turn left downhill. Go straight across the roundabout and down the A760 to Lochwinnoch. Go past the railway station on your left and the RSPB centre on your right. This has free entry to the nature centre and gift shop. Visiting the nature centre trails and hides is charged for unless you are an RSPB member. It is open daily from 10.00 to 17.00.

Continue on past Castle Semple Watersports, keeping the River Calder on your right. The riverbank here is a mass of ramsons (wild garlic), which are edible. Go under the railway path bridge and turn right over the river into Main Street. The sign is for 'Lochwinnoch, Kilmalcolm B768 and Castle Semple, Muirshiel'. About 100 metres up on your right is the Brown Bull.

23. Houston

Route: Houston—Craigends—Kaimhill Farm—Bridge of Weir—Kilmalcolm—Killellan — Barfillan

Distance: 9 miles

Map: OS Landranger 64, Glasgow; OS Lanranger 63, Firth of Clyde

Start: Fox and Hounds, Houston

Access: There is a regular bus service from Glasgow. Phone 0141 636 3195, or Dart Buses on 0141 889 0811. By car: take the M8 westbound out of Glasgow towards the airport. Come off at junction 28a and directly on to the A737 for Irvine and Dalry. About two miles along here turn left on to the B789, marked Houston. Go right immediately at a roundabout and straight through a second roundabout. Drive directly ahead through another roundabout and cross the A761 a couple of hundred metres further on. After about two miles turn left at a fourth roundabout onto the B790 for Bridge of Weir. Approximately two hundred metres along here turn right (no roundabout) at the sign for Houston. About 50 metres after this go straight through a fifth roundabout. The Fox and Hounds is about two hundred metres down this road on your right. Turn right into South Street at the near edge of the pub, and after 20 metres the car park entrance is on your left. It is a good-sized car park.

Fox and Hounds

Do not enter this pub if you are a member of the League against Cruel Sports. It will be your worst nightmare come true. There are stuffed foxes, mounted animal heads, hunting decor and accoutrements galore. Also the Lanarkshire and Renfrewshire Hunt meets here regularly. On the other hand, if you are neutral or pro-hunting this is a pub out of the top of the top drawer. It has everything: a beautiful setting, gorgeously decorated and furbished interior, excellent food and a range of real ales including the products of their own micro-brewery.

This is a listed building built in 1773. It was originally called the Black Bull. It was one of a string of coaching inns stretching from Lanarkshire to Renfrewshire and all called the Black Bull. The Travel

Lodge of the day. Upstairs, where the Huntsman Restaurant is now, there was accommodation and the Stable Bar is where the stables were. In 1820 it became the Fox and Hounds. Subsequently it has been Renfrewshire's CAMRA pub of the month and the Scottish *Sunday Mail's* pub of the month.

Inside there is much to see. I have only space to mention the highlights. The wallpaper and upholstery feature hunting scenes. There are horns, stirrup cups, horses' collars etc. The Stables Bar has a stuffed crocodile on its ceiling and murals of maps of old Houston around 1900 on its walls. There are also rugby cartoons around the pool table. From the Fox and Vixen Bar you can look into the micro-brewery.

Landlord Carl Wengel is delighted to see walkers. Children are welcome in the Huntsman's Restaurant and the back bar of the Fox and Vixen until 20.00. During beer festivals there is usually something on for kids such as face painting. There can be up to 15 real ales on offer at these times. There are normally two resident ales from the micro-brewery, Killellan (3.7 per cent ABV, a pale ale) and Barochan (ABV 4.1 per cent, a darker ale with a touch of roasted barley flavour) plus two to four guest ales. Keg products include Calders Cream Ale, Carlsberg Export, Carlsberg Lager and Dry Blackthorn Cider. Opening hours are Monday to Friday 11.00 to 24.00, Saturday 11.00 to 23.45 and Sunday 12.30 to 23.00.

Downstairs in the Fox and Vixen and Stables Bars there are only soup and sandwiches on offer. Upstairs in the Huntsman Restaurant, bar meals are served as well as a full à la carte menu. They also supply real ale here. Food speciality de la maison is seafood but a wide range of traditional Scottish fare is also available. There is a small vegetarian choice. On Sunday two traditional roasts are available. Food is served seven days a week. Weekdays it is 11.00 to 14.30 and 17.30 to 22.00. At weekends food is on offer all day to 22.00. Telephone 01505 612448/612991.

Houston

The original name of Houston was Kilpeter (Cillpeter), the cell of St Peter. It became called Houston (Hughstoun) when it was feued to Hugo de Padvinan in the 12th century. He built a castle here. This was a classic medieval castle with turrets, four thick, square walls, a moat, drawbridge and portcullis. In the reign of Alexander III (1249-1286) this

Market Cross, Houston

castle was ranked in importance with Edinburgh, Stirling and Dumbarton. Houston grew up around this castle. Houston House of the present day is on the site of this castle. In fact, its west wing is part of the original castle. The original wall of Houston Castle that separates it from the house is seven metres thick. It has a completely enclosed stairway inside it.

The Houstons were lairds here for 500 years, but in 1752 the Houstons of Houston became extinct. The estate was acquired by a Mr Macrae. He had been adopted as a ragged orphan in the streets of Ayr by a Hew M'Quire, who educated him. Later Macrae became Governor of Madras. In gratitude he bought the Houston Estate for Hew M'Quire's grandson James in 1748, on condition that he took the name Macrae. James Macrae's son James was obsessed with guns and gunpowder.

He blew up most of Houston Castle with gunpowder. He also disturbed the peace of St Peter's fair in Houston by shooting patterns in the tailboards of carts with pistols, like a spaghetti western. He left the country after shooting dead his opponent in a duel. But before he left he laid out the new village that forms the basis of today's Houston. He gave the villagers free stone from the old castle for their new houses, some 35 in total. He died in Prussia. There was a great deal of village rebuilding at the end of the 18th century. This was known as the planned village movement.

Killellan

At a seminary in Bangor on Belfast Lough in the 7th century there was a student named Fillan. From here, after graduation, he went to join his uncle Comgan in Whithorn, Galloway. Disagreements between the native Celtic Christians and the incoming Romans led to them going to Dornie in Inverness-shire. Later Comgan went to Turiff and Fillan went south to join the monks at Paisley. He stayed long enough in the Killin/Tyndrum area for it to be named Strathfillan.

After fording the Clyde he arrived at Killellan (pronounced Killallan – 'the cell of St Fillan') and was so taken with the place that he made it his residence thereafter. He lived and worked here until his death in 749. St Fillan's Well at the foot of the hill near Killellan Church is reputed to be a healing well, especially for bairns with rickets.

The Walk

Leave the Fox and Hounds by the door at the micro-brewery. Turn right uphill past the Cross Keys. Walk past the war memorial on your left and Old Schoolhouse Lane on your right. Take the first road on the right after this. This is called Kilmalcolm Road. Go past Cricketfields Lane and Fields Lane on the right. At the T-junction at the bottom go left along Kirk Road. Follow this road around to the right. Just before the church on your left is the access to Houston House. If you sneak 10 metres up the driveway you can get a peek at it. At the slightly offset four-way junction at the end of Kirk Road take the left-hand road. At the main road some 300 metres along go left of the chevrons on the pavement. Just before the pavement ends, turn right, cross the road and go up Ardgryffe Crescent straight ahead of you. Keep with this as it bears right. At Riverside on the left you will find a concrete footpath leading to a footbridge over the River Gryfe. Renfrewshire used to be called Strathgryfe. This comes from two Welsh words: 'ystradd' (valley) and 'gryf' (strong or rapid).

Once across the footbridge stay on the concrete path as it bears right. This path becomes beaten-earth then concrete and beaten-earth again. Follow this path for about half a mile, keeping the River Gryfe on your right. Bypass a concrete walkway on the left and a footbridge on the right. Eventually the footpath becomes narrower but is still easily discernible. The woods fall away on both sides of you as you approach the B789 road – ahead of you across grass. Go directly across the B789 and up the minor road in front of you. Keep on this road for about half a mile until it bends left where a very minor road goes straight ahead. Bear left and stay with this road for another quarter of a mile until a bridge crosses the road. Just before the bridge, on your left, is the access ramp to the disused railway line path. Go up here and double back to your right along the railway line path. In the summer there can be yellowhammers singing here, a little bit of bread and no cheeeese!

Follow this railway line path for the next three and a half miles. There are various plaques by the path giving you information about places along the route. There are also trackside sculptures at mile markers. Cross the viaduct over the River Gryfe. Go under a number of bridges and through a dyke across the path. Go **over** a road and a cart track on bridges then bypass a path to the right by a red sandstone football pitch. This is after the 18-mile marker. At this point the village of Kilmalcolm is visible beside you. Kilmalcolm means 'the cell of St

Columba'. This is reflected in the local pronunciation of the name as 'kilmacomb'. A couple of hundred metres past the football pitch path is a bridge **over** the railway line path. A board here gives you some details of Kilmalcolm.

Turn right up Station Road here. At the top go left at the T- junction. When you arrive at the main Port Glasgow Road go directly across it into Marketplace. After about 20 metres walk right and proceed up Gillburn Road. Keep along here as a road comes in from the right and follow it left to a bridge. Just before the bridge go right onto Gowkhouse Road. Bear left along here past the manse in front of you. Then bear right and left with this road and go up through woods, ignoring a driveway doubling back to the left.

Passing several driveways on your left, this now unmade road takes you up to a sign on the left – 'Public Footpath to the Houston and Killellan Road'. A board tells you about the nature reserve along here. Where this path forks, follow it right along the edge of the wood. The marsh on your left is Glenmoss. This path leads to a boardwalk. On your left here you may see the white fluffy heads of cotton grass. At the end of the boardwalk take the right-hand path to the golf course and follow the edge of the trees on your right around to the left. When the trees end go right up the unmade road by the old cottage. Just before the minor tarmac road walk up the right-hand edge of the fairway to your left, keeping close company with the wall on your right. Just past the trees on your right an obvious path through the rough ahead leads you to a footpath sign. Go right to and left along the minor road here.

About a mile along this road, some two hundred metres before it enters woodlands, is the hamlet of Killellan. This is where St Fillan lived and gives its name to the Fox and Hounds beer. There is nothing here now but the old manse and the ruined kirk.

Along this stretch of road in summer you will see many foxgloves. An extract from these, digitalis, is a powerful heart medicine in current use. So there might be something in the old witches' incantations, 'Eye of newt, toe of frog, glove of fox'?

There are good views of West Central Scotland from up on this road. About a mile after the woodlands there is a four-way junction with 30 mph signs, take the right-hand road here. About 200 metres down here on your left is the Fox and Hounds.

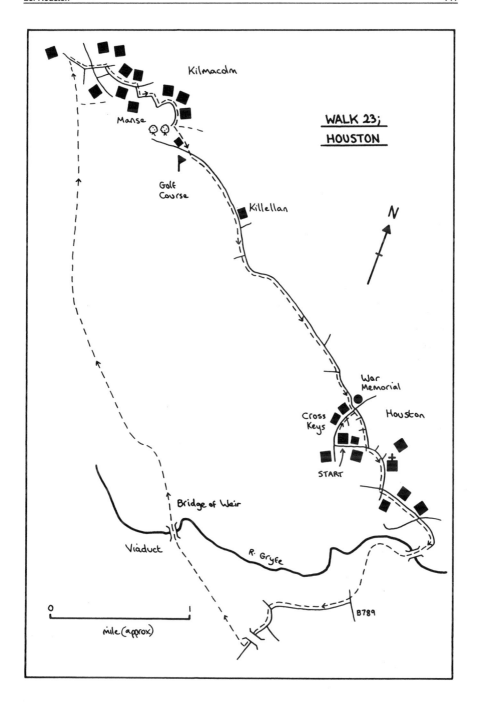

Kilmacolm

Manse

Golf
Course

Killellan

WALK 23;
HOUSTON

N

War
Memorial

Cross
Keys

Houston

START

Bridge of Weir

Viaduct

R. Gryfe

B789

0   1
mile (approx)

24. Glenniffer Braes

Route: Barrhead — Brownside — Glenpark — Braemount — Thornliemuir — Capellie — Killock — Woodneuk.

Distance: 6 miles

Map: OS Landranger 64, Glasgow

Start: The Crossed Stobs, Barrhead

Access: Barrhead is on the south-western edge of Glasgow, just across the city boundary in Renfrewshire. Paisley is just to the north-west of Barrhead. To avoid confusing one-way systems and ambiguous signs I would suggest that drivers coming from Glasgow adopt the following route. Take the M77 towards Ayrshire until junction 2. There go westward on the B762 for Barrhead. This merges with the A736 for Barrhead. However, do not follow this into Barrhead. Instead turn right on the A726 for Paisley. About two miles along this turn left on the B771 for Barrhead. This comes to a junction with the B774. The Cross Stobs is on the near left-hand corner of this junction. Turn to the left to find unrestricted parking on the main road. By train: there is a regular half-hourly weekday train service from Glasgow to Barrhead. Telephone 0345 484950. In Barrhead Station go downstairs and under the railway to emerge on the main road. Here turn right and the Crossed Stobs is about a quarter of a mile up on the right. There are also plenty of buses — telephone 0141 636 3195.

The Cross Stobs, Barrhead

Standing, as it does, at the junction of two roads, it is no surprise to learn that the Cross Stobs originated as a coaching inn. The public bar has been serving the Ayrshire to Paisley traffic for 275 years. The other parts of the building were houses subsequently converted to licensed premises. The public bar has a real fire and is attractively decorated in light plasterwork and dark wood. The comfortable lounge has leather chesterfields and a dining area. There is a beer garden at the rear. Other attractions include a pool table and free newspapers.

The name Cross Stobs originates from *stabs*, which are stakes in the ground like fenceposts. Landlord James Galbraith is happy to see walkers as is evinced by the fact that rangers from Gleniffer Braes Country Park use this as a start/finish point for conducted walks in the park. The rangers' number is 0141 884 3794.

There were two real ale handpumps dispensing Orkney Dark Island and Belhaven Five Nations when I was there. Other pumps pour Tennents Lager, Tennents 80/-, Tennents Velvet 70/-, Tennents Special, Caffreys, Guinness and Blackthorn Cider, both dry and sweet.

The pub also offers doubles of gin, vodka and Grant's Whisky for less than the price of a pint. There is a good selection of food for lunchtimes (only) Monday to Saturday from 12.00 to 14.30. If there are a crowd of you going on a Sunday and you phone in advance they will be happy to supply food for you. The opening hours are from 11.00 to 24.00 Monday to Thursday and Saturday. On Fridays it is open to 01.00. On Sundays the pub hours are 12.30 to 24.00.

The pub car park is currently closed as it is being disputed. It is hoped that it will be open again in the near future. Meanwhile parking on the main road is unrestricted. Telephone 0141 881 1581.

The Cross Stobs Inn

Gleniffer Braes Country Park

The name Glenniffer comes from Glen o'Firs, 'fir' being the old Scottish word for a Scots pine. The hill is of Clyde Plateau Lava laid down some 350 million years ago. It is a park of some 520 hectares (1300 acres) and is mainly moorland with some hill farming and forested areas. Interesting wildlife includes hen harriers and black grouse. The black grouse is a large bird of up to some four and a half feet long. The female has the descriptive name of greyhen. The best time to see these normally shy birds is on a spring morning around dawn when the males gather for establishment of dominance and mating rights on ancestral display grounds called leks. Their favourite winter food is birch buds.

The land was inhabited in ancient times as is evidenced by stone grain-drying kilns and clearance cairns in the park. In those days beasts would have been driven up to summer pastures on the hilltop, rather as is done today in alpine regions of Europe. The cowherds lived in stone-walled, turf-roofed buildings called sheilings.

The east end of the park was formerly part of the Paisley Royal Stewart Hunting Forest. At various times some of Scotland's best-known landowning families have held this land including the Wallaces, the Earls of Abercorn, the Earls of Dundonald and the Dukes of Hamilton.

But Gleniffer is best known for its intimate associations with the Paisley Weaver Walker Poets, Robert Tannahill (1774-1810) and Hugh MacDonald (1817-1860). Both of these poets frequently walked across, drew inspiration from and wrote about Gleniffer Braes. It is thought that the nature of their tasks gave them time to muse. Indeed, Robert Tannahill kept a slate on his loom for scribbling things down as they occurred to him. Between 1874 and 1935 annual concerts were held in Gleniffer Braes to commemorate the works of these poets. Crowds of up to 30,000 attended and choirs of up to 500 sang the poets' creations.

The Walk

Come out of the Cross Stobs and cross the B771 Grahamston road to go up Caplethill Road, the B774. Cross Caplethill Road and walk up it towards the bus stop and the end of speed limit signs. About a quarter of a mile along here, where the pylons cross the road, take the farm road on the left signposted for Glenniffer Braes Country Park. Go to the left of the farm and about 100 metres past it a signpost directs you right on a footpath to Glenpark. Brownside Farm is shown as existing in 1654 by cartographers of the era. There was once a mill here.

At the T-junction at the top follow the signpost pointing you right to Glenpark. Go over a stile and contour along the hillside. On your right is the town of Paisley. Cross a stile into woodland and turn left along a path, keeping to the high ground with the rhododendrons on your close left. Notice the woodland sculpture down on your right. This is Glenpark, where the open-air concerts were held.

When you reach a fence with palings and a millpond on your right, go left uphill on the semi-tarmac road. As the path becomes beaten-earth you arrive at a fork, take the steps uphill. A sign on your right guides you down to a waterfall, if you wish to see it, it is not very far to go.

Continue on past the waterfall sign, cross a footbridge and turn left at a T-junction. Cross another footbridge and immediately over this turn right along the bank of the burn. Bear left along a very minor road for about 50 metres, go through a gate and turn left up the metalled road to the golf club. Braehead car park is directly opposite you as you reach the golf club road. Go straight up this road, following signs for Paisley Golf Club. The road follows the path of an old coach road. Just after the sign for the professional's shop, take the stile on the left.

Go through the ten-metre wide belt of trees and turn right up the path on the other side. A cart track now appears. Follow the track up, keeping the trees on your near right. Follow this path into woods and out of them onto the moor. Walk along the cart track that bears right. Go through a gate and cross a ruined drystone dyke. Once over the dyke take the path that veers right following the line of the pylons. This bears to the right of the pylons and brings you to a fenced/dyked grassy path, turn left down this. At the end go over the stile and straight ahead, keeping the fence on your close left.

Follow the fence round to the right and at the field end you will come to a stile on your left. There is a sign here for Clyde Valley Community Forest, Thornliemuir Wood. Proceed straight ahead and downhill on the farm road. At the junction turn left through the gates and farm. Follow the farm road ahead and then around to the right. Go straight ahead on the tarmac road at the end of the farm road then go round to the left on it.

The valley of the Levern Water and the village of Neilston are now visible on your right. In 1830, at the peak of the cotton business, a

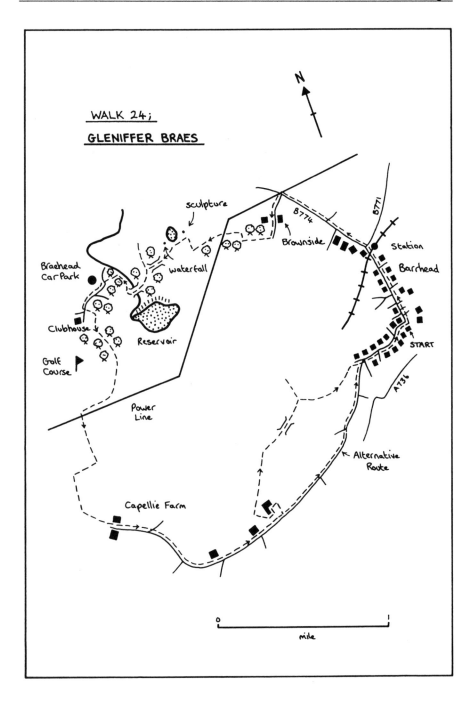

WALK 24;
GLENIFFER BRAES

two-mile stretch of the Levern Water had seven large mills, six printworks and numerous bleachfields. One mill still survives, producing sewing thread.

Just past Broomhead cattery along this road a path on your left allows you to view Killoch Glen waterfalls. These waterfalls were immortalised in verse by Robert Tannahill. About 200 metres past this, go **into** the courtyard of the farm buildings then left in front of the barn and around the farm onto the track up the hill. If you do not want to climb the hill, the road you are on will lead you into Barrhead at the railway station. Where you should turn left for the Crossed Stobs.

If you are continuing with the walk, go through a gate behind the farm and uphill. There is a farm gate at the top and the track forks just beyond it. You should turn right immediately before the gate up a wide, fenced, grassy area. At the top go over the fence to the right of the gate (easy climb) and turn right along a path parallel with the fence. This then veers left uphill and past a cairn on a hilltop to a stile/gate. This has had barbed wire across it but when I was there it had been cut. From here go slightly right over a small knoll and a cart track should become visible ahead. Go over the footbridge and along this track. When this track forks, go right to the rough road coming down from the transmitter mast. Go downhill on this, ignoring one bearing off to the right. At the bottom of the hill bear left onto Gateside Road. At the main road you will see the railway station. Turn left along the main road here and the Crossed Stobs is about a quarter of a mile along on your right.

25. Eaglesham

Route: Eaglesham – Low Hill – Picketlaw Reservoir – Bonnyton Moor – North Moorhouse – South Moorhouse – East Moorhouse – The Orry

Distance: 8 miles

Map: OS Landranger 64, Glasgow

Start: Cross Keys, Eaglesham

Access: By car: from the centre of Glasgow take the M8 westbound to junction 22. Here take the M77 towards Kilmarnock and Ayr. Go off at junction 3 and go left on the A726 for East Kilbride. Go straight through Eastwood Toll roundabout. Go under Williamwood railway bridge. Keep straight ahead at the Clarkston Toll roundabout. Go right at the Sheddens roundabout, on the B726 signposted for Eaglesham. About three miles along this road you will come to Eaglesham. Go into the centre of the village on this road and, just after the village green and Eglinton Arms Hotel on your right, you will come to a set of traffic lights. Go right at these lights on the B764 towards Kilmarnock. Then turn immediately left after the church and before the Cross Keys. The car park entrance is about 40 metres up this street on your right. There are regular bus services from Glasgow to Eaglesham, contact the Travel Centre on 0141 636 3195.

The Cross Keys, Eaglesham

The landlord, Mr MacDonald, thinks that this pub dates back to 1703. The first reference I can find for it is in 1747-55 when General Roy's military map of the area features the Cross Keys. General Roy, born in Carluke, was the founder of the modern-day Ordnance Survey. The pub was feued to Robert Montgomerie in 1773. In 1830 Hugh Montgomerie of the Cross Keys was treasurer when Eaglesham set up a committee (yes, even back then they had committees) to hold an annual cattle show. Notice that these landlords were Montgomeries of the ancient family of this village. It is a listed building, category B, of architectural or historic interest. In Eastwood District's list of buildings for Eaglesham Parish it is listed as a two-storey inn in painted stucco, lined up with ashlar, slated roof and symmetrical façade with dentilled cornice. Walkers will find a haven here.

It is a pub with a happy atmosphere. It has a collection of Clydesdale horse brasses. And I am glad to say it serves whisky in proper quarter of a gill measures, not the normal pathetic dribble in the bottom of a glass, which you have to gulp down, hastily for fear that it might evaporate before your eyes. It also serves real ale. The real ales are changed every week. When I was there the real ales were Morlands Old Speckled Hen, Belhavens St Andrew''s and Broughton Breweries Black Douglas. Keg barrels produce Belhaven Best, John Smiths, Tennents 80/-, Tennents Lager, Smooth Draught Lager, Caffreys, Guinness, Dry Blackthorn Cider and Ciderparty.

The excellent food is a cut above the normal pub lunch but not excessively priced. It is all made with fresh produce apart from frozen chips which is par for the course these days. If you want a more formal meal there is a restaurant upstairs which seats 95 people. The pub is open 11.00 (Sundays 12.30) to 24.00 seven days a week and serves food 12.00 to 14.30 and 18.30 until 22.00 everyday. Children are welcome until 20.30. Telephone 01355 302356.

The Cross Keys, Eaglesham

Eaglesham

Eaglesham is a picturesque village. In the 12th century Eaglesham was part of the lands granted by King David I to Walter Fitzalan, his steward. He gave Eaglesham to his friend Robert Montgomerie, whose family was in this estate in later centuries. John de Montgomerie took Henry Percy, Hotspur, prisoner with his own hands at the Battle of Otterburn in 1388. With the ransom or poind money he built the castle of Polnoon (Poinoon) just to the south of Eaglesham.

The name Eaglesham has a number of possible derivations. It could mean place of eagles as there could have been eagles here in medieval times and there is an eagle on the church spire next to the Cross Keys. It could also have come from the Gaelic 'eaglais' – a church. Or it could have been corrupted from Ecclesiasholm, meaning 'church in the hollow'.

The 12th Earl of Eglinton built the present village of Eaglesham in 1796 as a spinning and weaving village. A cotton mill was built but it burned down and was never rebuilt. The houses on the opposite sides of *The Orry*, the village green, have doors opening directly onto the street and the original long, narrow gardens at the back that were known previously as 'Lang Riggs'. These are listed by an Outstanding Conservation Area order.

Two miles north of the village on the road to Newton Mearns is the farm of Floors. It was here in 1941 that an astonished farm labourer found the lunatic Rudolph Hess who had landed by parachute from his plane. The story that this farmhand used a pitchfork is nice but not true. Hess was apparently hoping to sort out the current Anglo-German difference of opinion, otherwise known as the Second World War, by a few words with the Duke of Hamilton. I wonder if Hess said, 'Take me to your leader'?

The Walk

Turn right out of the Cross Keys and right again up the street between the church and the pub. If you look up at the church steeple you will see the eagle on top of it. Go past the car park and straight ahead, keeping the small black and white cottages on your left. After about 200 metres, where the road bears to the right, follow the footpath directly ahead. Pass through a stile on your left and follow the hedge on your right until the end of the field. Here go through a gap in the fence by the hawthorns and double back on the cart track on your right.